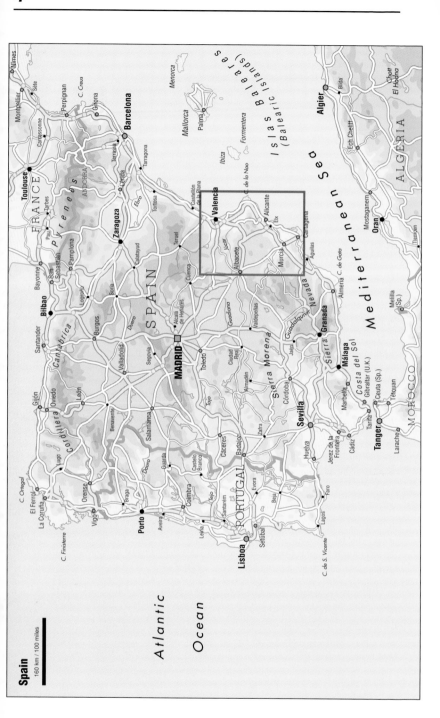

Spain
160 km / 100 miles

INSIGHT POCKET GUIDE

Costa Blanca

APA PUBLICATIONS
Part of the Langenscheidt Publishing Group

Welcome

This guidebook combines the interests and enthusiasms of two of the world's best-known information providers: Insight Guides, who have set the standard for visual travel guides since 1970, and Discovery Channel, the world's premier source of nonfiction television programming. Its aim is to bring you the best of the Costa Blanca, famous for its blue skies, white beaches and warm Mediterranean waters. The book covers not only today's Costa Blanca – the Alicante coastline – but also the southern stretch that was once part of it, and now has its own identity and popularity as the Costa Cálida.

In a series of tailor-made itineraries devised by Insight's correspondent, Vicky Hayward, we take you behind the cosmopolitan coast to explore the "real" Spain in the hinterland of the Alicante and Murcia regions: fertile valleys, historic towns, spectacular sierras and fine baroque architecture. The itineraries are divided into three sections; The North, covering the northern areas of Alicante region and southern Valencia; The Centre, which details the rest of Alicante region; and The South, which covers the Murcia region. There is also a section on leisure activities, including shopping, eating and drinking, nightlife, beaches and sport; and a practical basics section with a list of recommended hotels. With the use of Valenciano as well as Castilian Spanish in the region, there are variant spellings for some towns – a full explanation of spellings used in this guide can be found on page 96.

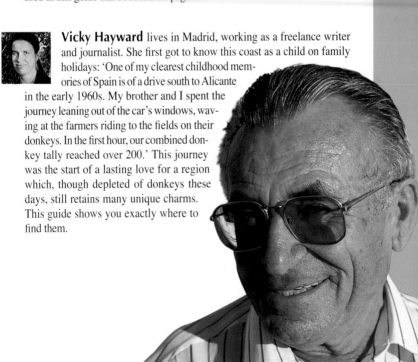

Vicky Hayward lives in Madrid, working as a freelance writer and journalist. She first got to know this coast as a child on family holidays: 'One of my clearest childhood memories of Spain is of a drive south to Alicante in the early 1960s. My brother and I spent the journey leaning out of the car's windows, waving at the farmers riding to the fields on their donkeys. In the first hour, our combined donkey tally reached over 200.' This journey was the start of a lasting love for a region which, though depleted of donkeys these days, still retains many unique charms. This guide shows you exactly where to find them.

HISTORY AND CULTURE

THE NORTH

THE CENTRE: ALICANTE REGION

Preceding Pages: the hilltop village of Polop de la Marina
Following Pages: local seafood specialities

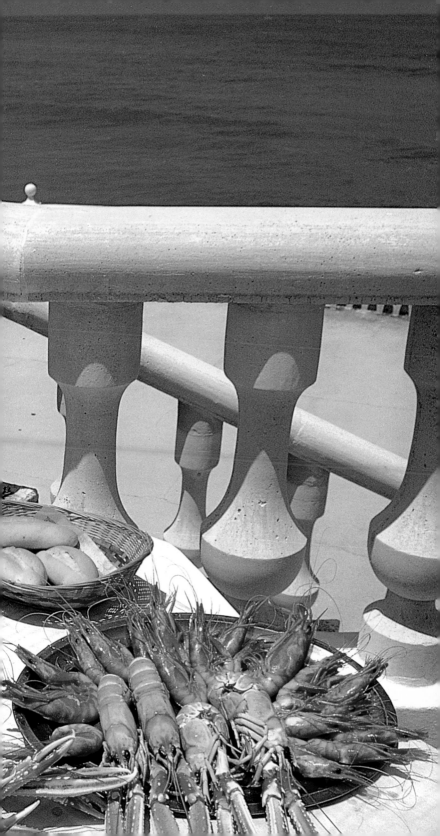

History
& Culture

The first evidence of human settlement in southeast Spain goes back to the Palaeolithic era, when man lived mainly on the fringes of the Cantabrian mountains and close to the eastern coast. In the range of low sierras between Alcoi and Yecla, a series of sites trace the evolution of what seems to have been a sizeable local population. Evidence dates from the early cave sites of around 50,000BC, through to more recent caves (*circa* 6,000BC) with paintings of hunting and animals (as at La Sarga, near Alcoi, and Monte Arabí, at Yecla) – to the walled towns of Iberian culture.

The Iberians' origins are obscure, but archaeologists have established that, by the 6th century BC, they were spread through present-day Valencia, Albacete and Murcia, living as autonomous tribes in walled towns. Two Bronze-Age cultures developed alongside one another: the Argaric to the south and Valencian to the north, with their boundary along the Vinalopo valley. Both used precious metals such as copper, silver, iron and gold to make ornaments and jewellery: examples can be seen at Villena and Cigarralejo.

Iberians, Phoenicians and Romans

The Argaric and Valencian cultures merged to become the Contestani. A farming people who kept large herds of cattle and grew wheat, they had good relations with the traders who came to their shores. The Phoenicians, who arrived in the 8th century BC, mined in the sierras and introduced fish-salting, the potter's wheel, the date palm, vine, fig and olive. Then, in the 5th century BC, the Massiliot Greeks charted the coast and built settlements along it. Adapting these Mediterranean influences, the Iberians produced fine decorated ceramics and sculptures, including the *Dama de Elche*, one of a series of stone carvings linked to the worship of a mother/fertility goddess.

After the western Phoenician colonies lost the first Punic War, they extended their power in southern Spain, triggering Iberian resistance and, in 218BC, Roman invasion. Under Publio Cornelio Scipio, the army moved slowly south from present-day Catalunya, nine years later conquering the Carthaginian capital Quart Hades, which the Romans renamed Cartago Nova – today Cartagena.

Here in Hispania Citerior – later Tarraconensis – Roman generals wintered, fish-salting factories were built, a road network was developed, irrigation systems were set up and large quantities of wine, olive oil and wheat were produced for export to Rome. The lead and silver mines behind Cartago Nova employed 40,000 Iberian slaves. Great tracts of forest, chopped down to provide timber, were replaced by *esparto* grass (used to make bags) and the city was renamed Cartago Espartaria.

Left: 16th-century map of the region
Right: the *Dama de Elche* stone carving

By the 4th century Christianity was generally accepted in Spain. In the decline before the collapse of Roman power in the 5th century, many towns were either abandoned and replaced by rural settlements, or changed site, moving – like Lucentum (Alicante) – to more defensive positions. Initially, most of this area was controlled by the Byzantines, but by the middle of the 7th century it had fallen, like the rest of the country, to the Visigoths.

The Arab Conquest

Just as the Romans had invited the Visigoths to help them keep order, so a dynastic Visigothic squabble opened the door to a Muslim takeover of the peninsula in 711–14. Tribes and dynasties from various parts of the Arab world invaded and ruled in succession. Meanwhile the power structure shifted from a potent caliphate, set up in Cordoba in the 8th century, to the *taifas*, or splinter kingdoms of the 11th century, and then to military control by the Almoravids and Almohads – Berber tribes from the Atlas mountains who invaded in the 12th century.

The landscape was transformed by Muslim circular irrigation techniques. Their water wheels and irrigation channels in the river valleys allowed the widespread cultivation of oranges, lemons, almonds and rice, which still forms the basis of the region's agricultural economy. Under the *taifas*, the flowering of urban culture and craft workshops – paper manufacture and silk-making, boat-building and ceramics – was to provide the basis of the medieval urban economy and, much later, the region's first industries.

Rural hamlets (*quaryas*), called *alquerías* by the Spanish, were protected and controlled by a network of castles, and planned in a pattern that has remained to this day in the Ricote and Gallinera valleys. Murcia city, founded in the 9th century, acquired power as the head of a *taifa* stretching north to Alicante, and briefly became the capital of al-Andalus in the 13th century; Dénia, the second city of the region and capital of another *taifa*, grew to a population of around 50,000 and was a cultural centre. Orihuela and Alcoy – both with a large number of cloth and dye workshops – Xàtiva, Cocentaina

and Lorca became important as commercial and administrative centres.

When the Christian Reconquest finally started in the 13th century, it moved swiftly southwards in a two-pronged drive by Castile and Aragon, more often taking the form of local surrender pacts than military victories. The treaties carving up the new territories moved the Aragonese border south. The 1304 Treaty of Torrellas fixed the border for the next 500 years, dividing the old kingdom of Murcia in half, with Orihuela and the lower Segura valley passing to Aragon and the rump remaining for Castile.

As social history, the Reconquest was a much slower process, with resettlement continuing in uneven spurts until the 18th century. Most large towns had begun to take on less defensive

Left: watchtowers were well-used
in medieval times

profiles by the end of the 14th century. Separate Muslim and Christian quarters typically spilled down from the protection of the castle rearing above them (Cocentaina is the clearest surviving example of this layout, with the Raval and Villa still quite distinct). Churches, often on the sites of 'purified' mosques, usually took more than several centuries to build due to lack of funds. María in Alicante and the cathedral at Orihuela are good examples of spacious late Gothic elements overlaid by trimmings in florid late Isabelline Gothic and 16th-century Plateresque. In the countryside, vineyards were planted to meet the new demand for wine.

The palaces and castles reflected the growing division of the reconquered territories into señorial power blocs. The Marquesado de Villena, virtually a state-within-a-state owing allegiance to Castile, was the most powerful of these, but huge tracts of land were granted to other noble families too over the course of time: Onil, Ibi, Castalla and Albatera went to the Marqueses de las Dos Aguas from Valencia; Cocentaina, Callosa and Benidorm to the de Laurias from Catalunya; great chunks of Murcia to the Marqueses of Velez. Likewise, the southern frontier towns around the Sierra de Espuña were for centuries ruled by the Orders of the Knights Templar and Santiago. The privileges of such absentee landlords came to be bitterly resented.

Castile and Aragon United

It was well after the union of Castile and Aragon through the marriage of Isabella and Ferdinand (1474) that the nobility began to co-operate with the Church and state. Aragon's trades – cloth, metalwork, leather, furniture making and boat building – grew out of resourcefulness rather than primary materials; in Murcia, the silk industry and mines were thriving again, but agriculture was held back by the region's inherent aridity. The two areas

Top: typical Muslim terracing near Pego
Above: a fine example of Arab influence

shared many problems: plague epidemics decimated the population in the 17th century; and Berber piracy led to a fear of invasion and the building of watchtowers and fortresses on the coast (as at Santa Pola and Campello).

A further serious blow was the expulsion of the *moriscos,* the Muslims who had stayed after the Reconquest and provided an invaluable skilled workforce. At first their customs and language were tolerated, but from the early 16th century they became a scapegoat for economic problems. Growing enmity found ritual voice in forced conversions and, finally, in expulsion in 1609 by Philip III. Initially, the Murcian *moriscos* were exempted because of their importance to the economy, but a few years later they, too, were expelled. A long economic and cultural recession resulted and the region did not recover fully till the 18th century.

Shaping a Spanish Identity

With the drawn-out War of Succession of 1702–14 and the accession to the throne of Philip V – the first of the Bourbon monarchs – the political map was redrawn. Many cities and towns in Valencia, which had backed Charles, Archduke of Austria, lost their rights. In contrast, areas that had solidly supported the Bourbon cause, such as Murcia and Alicante, benefited from royal favour. In the century that followed, the economic potential of natural resources began to be realised for the first time since the Reconquest. Reservoirs, windmills and aqueducts were built to irrigate arid areas; forests were cleared to plant vines, olives and cereals; the lower Segura valley was drained to become fertile *huerta*. Workshops producing silk and other textiles flourished in both Murcia and Alicante, and, in the middle of the century, industrial techniques appeared in Alcoi. Public works programmes and Genoese traders helped the ports to develop; Cartagena became a major defensive arsenal; Alicante boasted Spain's third-largest volume of trade.

The region's new wealth and confidence was expressed in a massive building boom that incorporated a late flowering of baroque architecture.

Above: the marriage of Ferdinand and Isabella changed the course of history

Palaces and señorial houses acquired ornate façades; churches were topped by blue-tiled cupolas like teapot lids; Murcia, Lorca and Orihuela were remodelled, with a new synthesis of religious and secular space. A decorative flair – which also found expression in fiestas and costumes – represented a dynamic society with a growing influence from Castile.

Anarchists and Secessionists

Economic development and the creation of a new middle class continued through the 19th century. Progress was checked temporarily by the War of Independence against the French and an earthquake in the Segura valley, but it was quickened by the confiscation and redistribution of monastery estates. The provincial boundaries of the 1830s marked the beginning of Orihuela's decline and Alicante's rise as a local capital. Improved transport brought new markets for agricultural produce and the first tourists, while industrialisation was prevalent in Alcoi and Cartagena. During the first Republic of 1873, anarchist workers at Alcoi seized the town, killed the mayor and the Guardia Civil, while at Cartagena, cantonalists seeking regional secession introduced divorce and abolished the death penalty before being bombarded into submission. Mining wealth left its mark in some wonderful Modernist architecture, at Cartagena, Jumilla, Alcoi, La Unión and Novelda, where there is a small museum.

For all this, rural 19th-century life – uninterrupted by invasion, immigration or cultural exchange – maintained a local quality. The vineyard regions around Monóvar, Dénia, Yecla and Jumilla, which boomed briefly when phylloxera destroyed French vines; the poor fishing and smuggling villages, such as Benidorm or Torrevieja; the green *huerta* of the Segura valley, its adobe *barracas* periodically swept away by flooding; the harsh northern valleys, where life still centred on the old *morisco* hamlets; the southern Campo de Cartagena, where windmills drew up water and ground wheat – all these geographical pockets lived as worlds apart from one another.

As they became sucked into the international marketplace, an economic crisis engulfed the land. At the turn of the century, vineyards and olive groves were torn up to make way for citrus fruit and almonds. The poverty never became as desperate as that of the south – the wealth of the *huertas* and the shared inheritance system meant there were more property owners than labourers – but the flow of emigration to local cities, North Africa and Catalunya was steady and, in the bad years of the early 1930s, it rose to a flood.

When civil war broke out in 1936, Murcia and the Levante (eastern Spain) declared for Republicanism and sent brigades to the military fronts. At home, churches were looted, cities bombarded. The collectivisation of land followed apace. After the fall of Madrid and the Republican government in Valencia, the region fell to the Nationalists in 1939.

Right: church domes in Jijona

Tourism: New Horizons

The postwar decade under Franco's military dictatorship saw painfully slow reconstruction by an exhausted country. Not until the 1950s did the economy strengthen and the gap close between town and country, inland and coastal areas. Driving here in the late 1940s, Rose Macaulay wrote, 'This is a haunted shore: ghosts around each bay, each little town, each castled rock, whispering in the lap of waves and in the low rumour of the sea wind in the palms.' Just a decade later, the tourist invasion was underway.

The first real boom, with accompanying rampant property speculation, took place in the 1960s: skyscrapers replaced the old inns and the number of visitors to Alicante province shot up to over 3 million a year. Smaller but significant booms followed in the 1970s and 1980s, spreading down the coast to the Mar Menor and inland to the valleys and sierras. Apart from the transformation it wreaked on the landscape and local economy, tourism became a major cultural phenomenon in the 1960s, bringing in its wake social liberalisation and the creation of a new bourgeoisie long before Franco's death and the arrival of democracy in 1978.

Despite the pressure of tourism, industry and agriculture have continued to hold their own. Industry – partly based on traditional local crafts and partly imported with oil refineries and the like – provides work for more than a quarter of the population. And although agriculture is shrinking, it has thrived in the Murcian *huerta,* known as the market garden of Europe.

In the past decade, concern for the environment has emerged as a major issue. Local indicators of a mounting crisis – such as falling fishing catches, high levels of air pollution, widespread mountain fires, soil erosion and growing water shortages – have highlighted the importance of an ecological balance in an area that has long-struggled against natural disaster. The protection of large areas of countryside, stricter controls on heavy industry and official backing for 'green' tourism is likely to be followed by more radical changes, particularly to provide long-term water supplies. The recent past has also seen the revival of regional culture – language, fiestas, cooking, dance, crafts and music – alongside the dawn of a new electronic economy. With its decentralised economy, high proportion of foreign residents, high quality of life and multilingual society, this new Mediterranean arc of affluence is already the integrated Europe of which many politicians dream.

H I S T O R Y   H I G H L I G H T S

c50,000BC First evidence of cave dwellings (found in Cueva del Cochino, Villena; Cueva de las Calaveres, Benidoleig).

8th century BC Phoenician traders introduce the pottery wheel, the fig and the olive.

23 AD Quart Hades founded on site of Cartagena.

218–19 Roman army, under Publio Cornelio Scipio, conquers Spanish Mediterranean coast, from Emporias to the Carthaginian capital, Quart Hades, which they rename Cartago Nova.

AD555 Byzantine troops conquer Cartago, but lose all their territory to Visigoths by 624.

711–14 Muslims invade and conquer Iberian peninsula, except for areas in the northwest.

756 Caliphate of Córdoba founded.

1010–95 Taifa kingdoms in power (in this area, Dénia and Murcia).

1095 Almoravides, Berbers from the Atlas mountains, invade.

1160 Another Berber tribe, the Almohades, invade.

13th century The Reconquest moves southwards in a two-pronged drive by Castile and Aragon.

1243–4 Kingdom of Murcia ceded by Ben-Hud dynasty to Castile.

1238–48 James I of Aragon conquers northern Alicante.

1263 Muslim rebellion in Murcia is put down by James I of Aragon.

1276 Muslim revolt in Alicante finally quashed.

1304 The Treaty of Torrellas confirms Alicante's annexation of Castilian territory south to Mar Menor.

1361 Pedro the Cruel finally captures Alicante for Castile after repeated attempts. (His brother, Henry II of Trastamara, later returns it after Pedro's death.)

1474 Ferdinand and Isabella marry to unite Castile and Aragon.

1492 Fall of Muslim Granada. The expulsion of Spanish Jews.

1519 Revolt against nobility and persecution of *moriscos* (converted Muslims) in kingdom of Valencia.

1609 Expulsion of *moriscos*.

1702–14 Spanish War of Succession between Philip of Anjou (V) and Charles, Duke of Hapsburg.

1783 Death of Francisco Salzillo, baroque sculptor.

1808–12 War of Independence (aka Peninsular War) against the French.

1812 A Spanish constitution written.

1829 Earthquake destroys towns of Lower Segura valley.

1833–6 Present provincial borders are fixed: Villena, Dénia and Orihuela are included in Alicante province.

1858 The Alicante–Madrid railway line opens.

1862 Railway line from Madrid to Murcia city opens.

1873 First Republic: *cantanolismo* (secession) in Cartagena.

1888 In Cartagena, Isaac Peral builds what is claimed to be the world's first working submarine.

1936–9 Civil War: Alicante and Murcia remain Republican.

1939 Surrender to the Nationalists after fall of Madrid.

1960–71 Number of visitors annually to Alicante province rises from 950,000 to more than 3,750,000.

1982 Statutes of Autonomy of Valencia and Murcia regions (Alicante becomes Valencia's southern province).

1992 Spain becomes full member state of the European Union.

1995 Regional government elections: Partido Popular (conservative) wins power in Valencia and Murcia.

Left: sun, sand and sea at Benidorm

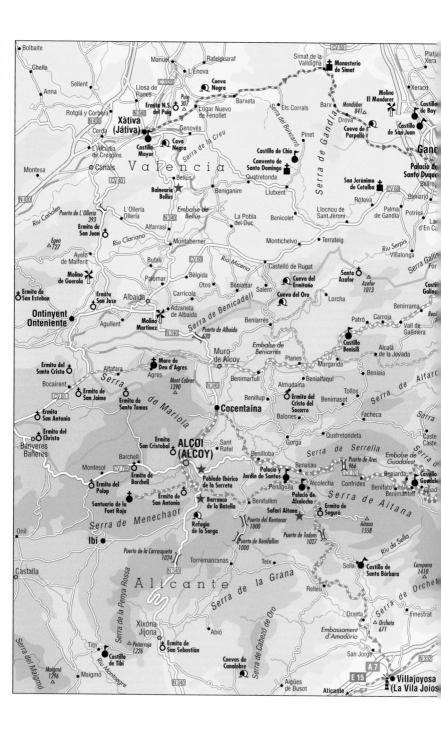

The North

1. EXPLORING THE NORTHERN COAST: CALPE TO THE COL DE RATES *(see map, p18–19)*

Allow 4 hours for the Peñón d'Ifach (a rocky coastal outcrop), the small town of Benissa and a beach. A leisurely drive (2½ hours with stops) loops back into wine country and up to a sierra viewpoint before dining at a country restaurant.

Dotted around the coastline of northern Alicante province, between the up-market family resorts and the ribbon of villas running between them, are unspoiled pockets with areas of lovely countryside. The towns and villages carry reminders of a long history of piracy and invasion. Start at **Calpe** (Calp), dubbed 'Muy Heroica Villa' by Charles V for its stoic defence against Berber pirates. Just outside the town, now a busy resort, is the **Peñón d'Ifach**, a huge limestone fang rearing out of the sea. Charted in ancient times and later used as a watchtower, it is now a symbol for the Costa Blanca, overlooking crowded beaches on either side but still keeping its splendid isolation.

The easiest parking place is in the fishing port below. From there it is a long climb up – the Peñón is 330m (1,083ft) high – through a tunnel in the bottom of the rock face (allow 30–40 mins). It is worth the effort though, since the views over the coastline are superb, especially if you can make it by sunrise. The slopes and rocky bays below are worth clambering over too; they are now a *parque natural* protecting over 300 plant species – including a unique orchid and carnation – which grow in the sheltered micro-climate. In summer, it is a good idea to return to the bottom before the heat of the day (the study centre has a convenient bar).

From the Peñón, cut back inland to **Benissa**, a town built several miles inland for safety from pirate attacks, with *rejas* (iron grills) over the windows. Everything of interest here is in one, long narrow strip running from the top to the bottom of the town. At the very top, in Calle Escoto, the Franciscan **Convento de los Capuchinos**, founded in 1611, is built of soft golden stone (ring on the doorbell to visit). Lower down, in the centre of town, the **Calle de la Purísima** is lined with lovely old medieval houses, often with old porches and gable designs of Muslim origin, and the 15th-century agricultural exchange houses a **Museu de Etnografía**, closed for restoration since 1998. Opposite you can pick up a late breakfast or mid-morning snack at a knock-out bakery, **Bolufer**.

Make your way back to the coast via Teulada and Benitachell, where smaller roads and tracks run down

Left: the Peñón d'Ifach rears out of the sea at Calpe
Right: a Costa Blanca letter box personified

past holiday housing to the beaches around the **Cabo de la Nao** and **Cabo San Antonio**. The most spectacular of these is the Cala de Moraig, an enclosed golden strip sheltered by tall cliffs reached through the Cumbre del Sol estate, which can only be described as a blot on the landscape. Less abrasive are **Platja de la Granadella**, further round, or the **Playa de Mar Azul**, looking over the tiny Isla de Portixol. It has good snorkelling, a diving pontoon and a couple of breezy beach bars.

Xàbia to the Gorgos Valley

Outside beach weather, it is easy to while away an hour or two in **Xàbia (Jávea)**. The town has a fine fortified Gothic church, its tawny stones softened and pockmarked by the salt winds. Nearby is the **Museo Arqueológico y Etnográfico** (Calle Primicias 1; Tues–Sun 10am–1pm and 6–9pm; July and Aug until 11pm; entrance fee), which explores the history of the coast from Palaeolithic caves and Iberian villages to Roman wealth and medieval poverty. It also has an excellent collection of Muslim ceramics and craft equipment, such as *alpargata* tools and a raisin press.

From here, it is a short drive up past the deserted terraces of the small **Serra del Montgó**, now a Natural Park, to the fish restaurants of **Dénia**. (As you come down into the bay take a sharp right, marked for Les Rotes, and then look for signs.) They are famed for their *arroz abanda*, rice cooked in a rock and shellfish stock flavoured with saffron and a sautéed tomato and onion *sofrito*. It may look plain next to most tourist *paellas*, but the flavour is wonderful. **El Pegolí**, one of several such restaurants, is particularly memorable *(see page 76)*. From here you can drive down to to **Les Roques**, the old fishing quarter, where the day's catch is auctioned at 5pm *(for more on Dénia see page 26)*.

In the late afternoon loop back into the olive and citrus groves, stopping off quickly for a glimpse of **Ondara's** wonderful small bullring, which sits on the northern edge of the town. Access is through the Bar Plaça de Bous: tickets for the fights, as well as concerts in summer, go quickly and need to be bought well in advance.

A short drive further on, at **Gata de Gorgos'** you turn off to **Llíber**, driving through rolling hills into the well-tamed wine country of the **Gorgos Valley**. As you approach **Xaló (Jalón)**, the soil turns from red to yellow and vineyards begin to cover the valley floor. They were once famed for their sweet malmsey and raisins made from muscatel grapes. Today the vineyards are still dotted by the characteristic *riu-raus*, arched porches used for drying the grapes, but they are hardly used. Xaló itself is a tranquil town dominated by a vast 19th-century church, with a good wine cooperative where you can taste and buy the claret-like red and excellent sweet muscatel wines. From here, drive on up to the **Col de Rates** – signposted for Tárbena and Callosa – a bare lookout point (780m/2,559ft) with great views.

Immediately below is **Parcent**, a dozy village where life rotates around the agricultural cooperative and its splendid *fin-de-siglo* bar. Stop off here for a local wine or *mosto* – unfermented grape juice – before backtracking to Llíber to finish the long day with supper at the **Terrases de la Torre**, a relaxed country restaurant serving excellent local dishes *(see page 76)*.

2. THE NORTHERN HILL TOWNS AND SIERRA DE AITANA *(see map, p18–19)*

A 1½ hour drive from the lush coast behind Benidorm takes you past a waterfall and hill villages to two inland towns with historic centres: Cocentaina and Alcoi. To see everything along the way, you need to make an early start or, for a leisurely day, make a choice of destinations before you start. The drive back crosses the Sierra de Aitana, with spectacular views.

In the northern sierras, all roads seem to lead to **Alcoi (Alcoy)**. Sited in a sheltered river plain where a number of rivers converge behind the coastal hills, it is both the oldest and largest of the northern hill towns, the original Iberian hill–top settlement looking down on textile and paper factories which grew out of Moorish workshops.

A first stop can be made at the **Fonts de Algar**, where the river of the same name rises just outside **Callosa de Ensarriá**. The road then runs on to Alcoi past Guadalest and Confrides. The lush frondiness drops away together with the sub-tropical micro-climate as the road winds between harsh sierras until you reach the chalky plateau of Alcoi. Just after Benilloba, take the right turn to **Cocentaina** (20 mins).

Above left: the steep slope of Benissa. **Left:** rooftops and skyline collide in Xàbia
Right: the faces of Spain's future

Cocentaina

One of the least written up but most interesting historic towns of the province, Cocentaina has clearly delineated medieval Christian and Jewish quarters on either side of the **Palau Comtal**, a 15th- to 16th-century fortified palace. After years of restoration, the palace is now open to the public (Mon–Sat visits at 10.30am and 12.30pm; July–Sept at 11.30am, 1.30 and 7pm; informal

guided tour, 30 mins, no charge). Long-term plans include the return of furnishings from the Casa de Pilate in Seville and museum space for the wealth of Iberian, Roman and Muslim finds made in the locality. In the meantime, the chapel with the *Mare de Déu*, a painting of the Virgin Mary said to have miraculously burst into tears, and some rooms with fine wooden ceilings and tiled floors, are fragments of the former magnificence of the palace.

The **Sala Dorada**, the Palau Comtal's most richly decorated room, situated on its western corner, is dedicated to the wartime victories of the Aragonese crown. The neighbouring **Convento de Clarisas** (7am–noon and evening Mass) is also worth a quick peep inside for its collection of fine paintings, which include a 15th-century Byzantine *retablo*.

Paraje San Cristobal, next to the hermitage of the same name, is an excellent place for a leisurely lunch. Dishes are substantial and in the after-lunch gap, when everything other than bars and restaurants is closed, you can sit over an *eau-de-vie*. A hot-weather alternative is a picnic at **Font Roja**, a 20-minute drive on the other side of Alcoi. The 19th-century chapel is superbly sited next to an icy water source and a former health spa converted into a government *parador*. From here, paths lead up into beautiful Mediterranean woodland with *carrascas* (kermes oaks) now protected as a natural park.

Alcoi

Late afternoon, when the streets are coming back to life, is the perfect time to arrive in **Alcoi**. As you approach from Cocentaina over the suspension bridge, the town's geography is at its most dramatic, with houses appearing to topple down into a gorge cut by the meeting of rivers. The town centre is quite distinct from others in the province, with a secular air reflecting its early industrialisation: hence the old-fashioned banks and shops (for example in **Calle Juan Cantó**), the frilly modernist balconies and workers' cultural centres, and the five bridges. All of these date from the end of the last century and were built with the profits from the cotton industry.

Above: doves flutter around the site of a demolished convent in Alcoi's Plaça de Dins

The open spaces are thoroughly 19th-century too. La Bandeja, as the main Plaça d'Espanya is known, is heavy and grandiose; but the smaller neighbouring **Plaça de Dins**, where doves flutter around over the site of the convent torn down in the 1820s, and the nearby **Glorieta**, a park with peacocks and a tall dovecote, are charming places to observe well-dressed provincial Spanish life.

Below the main square is the graceful, if down-at-heel, old core of the town. The 17th-century town hall houses the local archaeological museum; **Museu Arqueologic Municipal** (Mon–Fri 9am–2pm, Sat, Sun and holidays 10.30am–1.30pm. Closed July–Sept), whose exhibits include a small lead tablet with writing in an undeciphered Iberian alphabet and the Iberian Dama de Jerreta.

Nearby is the **Museu de Festes**, the private museum of the town's rumbustious Moors and Christians fiesta (C. San Miguel 60, Tues–Fri 11am–1pm and 5.30–7.30pm, weekends and holidays 10.30am–1.30pm; entrance fee). The pomp of the fiesta costumes and the paraphernalia that goes with them is extraordinary; to the people of Alcoi, it is a matter of both great pride and of economic interest, since many of the factories making these and costumes for this and other fiestas around the country are based here.

To return to the coast, take the mountain road over the **Sierra de Aitana** via the villages of Benifallim, **Penaguila** – worth a look – and **Relleu**, a lovely unspoilt village from which you can walk to an Arab castle (ask locally). There are paths up into the mountains, semi-alpine flora and some fine views here, plus a couple of bars where you can have a drink while watching the sun set and perhaps stay on for a homely supper.

Alternatively, extend your stay to spend several days exploring the walking country nearby in the Sierra Mariola, returning to the coast via the picturesque valleys of Gallinera, Alcalà *(see pages 27, 28)* and Ebo.

Above: the Moors and Christians fiesta in Alcoi

3. DÉNIA AND THE TRAIN SOUTH *(see map, p18–19)*

After exploring the pleasant town of Dénia, enjoy a relaxing train ride south to Alicante. Train details are on page 92.

Dénia's elegant air of old wealth makes it quite distinct from other resorts. 'Of all the lovely places down the Iberian seaboard, I believe Dénia…to be the most attractive,' wrote Dame Rose Macaulay. Perhaps it appealed to her so much because of the English colonial imprint left by raisin dealers who lived here from 1800 to the Civil War. The large, sweet raisins are no longer the heart of Dénia's economy, but they are still renowned for their quality (the Monday street-market by the station or the municipal market, Calle Carlos Senti are the most likely places) and one of the raisin warehouses stands on Calle Mar.

Five minutes' walk from the station are the shady main avenue and **Plaza de la Constitución**, where the 17th-century church (open during Mass) faces the *ayuntamiento*, tumbling with bougainvillaea and geraniums in summer. Inlaid in its Renaissance façade is a stone from the Roman **Temple of Diana** after which the town itself was named (the inhabitants of Dénia are still called *dianenses*).

Other monuments are the walls and towers of the **castle**, which was built by the troops during the siege of the Muslim town (one of the most important of the Mediterranean coast) and refortified during the War of Independence, when the French occupied the town for four years. Underneath runs a long tunnel cut through the rock, and inside is a small **archaeological museum** (the daily opening times vary: ask in the Tourist Information Office, tel: 96 642 2367). Close by, the small **Museo Etnologico** (Calle Cavellers s/n; Tues–Sat 10.30am–1pm, 4–7pm, Sun 10.30am–1pm only) has old photos of raisin-making, work tools and furniture. Another curiosity, which is found along the walk between

Above: the Museo Etnologico in Dénia
Left: Miguel de Cervantes, author of *Don Quixote*

the city centre beach, **Les Rotes** and the seafood restaurants, is the English cemetery, where raisin merchants and sailors were buried. One poignant tombstone survives in memory of 'Reginald Rankin, born 12th August 1864, died 3rd December 1865'. The walk to Les Rotes takes 25 minutes in all, bringing you to a series of idyllically quiet, small rocky coves.

The Lemon Express

From Dénia you can travel along the single-track railway which runs south to **Alicante**. Once known as the Lemon Express, it is an endearing hangover from the past, for an express train it is not: it makes 33 stops on a 50-mile journey in 2½ hours.

This is its great advantage, for you can reach many parts of the coast (and the countryside behind it) without getting bogged down in traffic and, at the same time, enjoy the scenery and watch the local passengers going about their daily business en route. You can also take your bicycle with you for only 50 pesetas extra. Seven trains run during the day, and in July and August the nightime train, known as the *Trensnochador*, runs right through till 5am in the morning to link the Costa's hectic nightspots. At weekends special tickets combine a train ride with a guided walk from one of the stations along the route. The most scenic stretch is between **Dénia** and **Calpe**, initially passing through lush citrus groves but soon entering the dry lands behind the coastal plain. Ferrandet and Xara (Jara) stations give access to hilly walking country in the Sierras de Montgó and Bérnia. The views here have changed less than you might expect since Rose Macaulay followed the same route by road in 1949, 'through strange ash-pale country, very dry, with little vines and olives, and huge, odd-shaped rocks and mountains'.

4. THE GALLINERA VALLEY: MORISCO VILLAGES AND CHERRY BLOSSOM *(see map, p18–19)*

The inland valley between Pego and Agres (total 1½ hours' drive without stopping), and the smaller Alcalà and Ebo valleys running off it, can be seen in a day, although a longer stay will be rewarding.

Nowhere is the contrast between the modernity of the coast and the traditional way of life inland so marked as it is in the **Vall de Gallinera** with its quiet agricultural villages, Muslim imprint and surrounding sierras. To get a proper feel for this region allow two to three days, leaving time to walk as well as drive. The springboard for the area is **Pego**, a bustling small town which has lost its rice fields but keeps the local architecture of farm villages. If the church is open for morning mass (9–10am) you will be able to see the fine 15th-century *retablo* of the pregnant **Virgen de la Esperanza** inside.

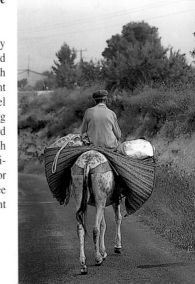

Right: life in the slow lane

From Pego, take the road to Planes (marked for **Muro de Alcoy** or **Muro del Comtat**) which follows the Vall de Gallinera. The traces of the converted Muslims who stayed after the Reconquest quickly show themselves: the terracing of the steeply banked hillsides, and then, after the road has run through a spectacular gorge, the Arabic names and layout of the old *alquerías*, or hamlets. Some of the more isolated villages – **Alcalà de la Jovada**, for example – even have deserted, dry-stone *morisco* ruins still standing. The area became a stronghold for rebellion: one revolt, led by the charismatic Al-Azraq, lasted from 1258–75; another was a dramatic last stand against expulsion in 1609 by 15,000 *moriscos*. Outnumbered, they eventually surrendered and were deported from Dénia the following spring.

Just before Planes, a track hairpinning down to the right signed for the **Barranc del' Encanta** ('enchanted ravine') leads to a wonderful blue swimming hole fed by a waterfall. From here you can walk along the valley between olive and citrus groves, or drive on up to the ruined castle at **Lorcha**.

Perched on a small hill below a ruined 12th-century castle, **Planes** keeps its medieval shape, a 17th-century aqueduct built for a long defunct dis-

tillery, the oldest fiesta in the province *(see page 84)* and a string of bars along the main road.

The Sierra de Mariola

It is only half-an-hour's drive from here to **Agres**, tucked into the side of its quiet valley. The **Pensión Mariola** *(see page 94)* makes a really comfortable, quiet rural base for the excellent walking country round about. Up on the **Sierra de Mariola**, there are medieval snow-wells in which ice was made for the summer, prehistoric caves and a large number of wild herbs (take the forest path up past the sanctuary, which is also worth a look). Down in the valley, a path leads along various stretches of the river and there is an old *balneario* or spa. A short drive on up the valley will also bring you to **Bocairent**, a quiet market town with a picturesque medieval quarter and a bullring carved into the rock.

An alternative route for your return journey takes you along the road to Alcalà de Jovada through the **Vall d'Ebo** and past the **Cova del Rull**, a cave full of spectacular stalactites and stalagmites (10.30am–8.30pm; Oct–Mar closes at 5pm). The valley's cherry blossom is a wonderful sight in April and May and the Vall d'Ebo cooperative sells the cherries in season, varietal honeys, almonds and olive oil. You can also eat very well at the Bar Piscina *(see page 77)*. On the final stretch to Pego, the road passes the spectacular Barranc del Infiern (literally Hell Gorge), accessible only to skilled climbers, then drops to the coast with splendid views along the way.

After all this, returning to the coast comes as a shock. One is left wondering how long the valleys can resist the development creeping up from the resorts.

Above: a medieval snow-well on the slopes of the Sierra de Mariola

5. THE GUADALEST VALLEY AND ALTEA
(see map, p18–19)

Allow 45 minutes driving time to Guadalest from the turn-off behind Benidorm, and the same to Altea. En route you will find a spectacular waterfall, a Muslim castle with panoramic views and lush medlar groves.

The **Guadalest Valley** is one of the most photogenic of Alicante province's landscapes, with tall peaks and hill villages above lush green valleys. Start in **Polop de la Marina**, a sleepy village with the tall mountain of **Ponoch** looming above it on one side. The main sight here is the Font Els Zorros, a modern extension of the old water fountain with 221 spouts. From here the village streets slope steeply up towards the deserted cemetery, built on the site of the ruined castle. There are fine views over the valley floor below and the surrounding peaks, often backed by swirling clouds.

The road continues to Callosa d'En Sarrià, where you turn off to the **Fonts de Algar** waterfalls (take the road to Tárberna and follow the signs; there is a large car park). Buried in a jungly-green valley filled with citrus and medlar groves, the water alternates between cascades and pools, running between river banks covered with pink oleander and bougainvillaea in summer. Starting at the lowest and most spectacular waterfall and natural bathing pool, you can climb up alongside the river for 20 minutes or so until it becomes a mountain stream and then, where the path runs out, wade on up to the top.

Up to the Castle

Return to Callosa and take the turning for **Benimantell**, which runs through medlar, almond and olive groves and gives you the best first view of the village of **Guadalest**, its castle and bell tower precariously balanced on fangs of rock rearing up from the valley. This was one of the Muslim network of castles which collected taxes and kept an eye on the scattered rural hamlets in these northern valleys. Now, the silhouette and view from the top of

Above: the Guadalest Valley

the castle are, in truth, its best points since the handful of streets are overrun with souvenir stalls and there is little to see except for the entrance arch to the town and the 12th-century dungeon. There is a small private museum of rural life here, the **Museo Etnológico** (10am–6.30pm, later in summer; closed Sat in winter), which recreates a late 19th-century farmhouse.

From here you can drive down through the neighbouring village of **Beniardá** and round the reservoir to the dam, before climbing up to the main road again. It is then half an hour's drive back to Callosa, winding round between groves of medlars and citrus trees, and dropping down to cross the river. In summer, oleander, bougainvillaea and purple convolvulus tumble around the roadside in glorious profusion.

From Callosa it is a short but winding drive down to **Altea la Vieja** (or **La Vella**), identifiable by its blue church dome. Carefully restored by the colony of artists who moved in during the 1950s, it is now hoping to become a miniature cultural capital thanks to the arrival of a new fine arts university, a major new concert hall and the **Centro Internacional de la Musica Villa Gadea** (Pda la Olla 26; June–Sept 8am–2pm, 5–9pm; Oct–May 8am–3pm, 4–8pm), set up by UNESCO as a home for five international music foundations. The centre has a changing exhibition of instruments from around the world, puts on open-air concerts in the summer, and has beautiful gardens running down to the sea. The café *terrazas* in the old town's attractive plaza are busy in the evening, with a good variety to choose from. Among them, the **Posada de San Miguel** (Calle Conde de Altea 24, tel: 96 584 0143) on the coast road, is a good choice for well prepared traditional dishes, such as *paella* cooked over a wood fire.

6. THE LAND OF THE BORJAS: XÀTIVA AND GANDIA
(see map, p18–19)

Allow 40 minutes' drive from the coast north to reach Xàtiva, home town of the Borjas, and another 2–3 hours to look around; in the afternoon, Gandía gives the option of town or beach.

The history of the Borjas (also spelled Borgias), is usually thought of as Italian because Rome was the base of their nepotism, power politics and sexual intrigues. From there Alfonso de Borja, Pope Calixto III, orchestrated the 15th-century campaign against the Turks, his nephew Alexander VI carved up the New World between the Spanish and Portuguese and his son,

Above: a cool spot for a drink on Altea's Plaza de la Iglesia

Caesar, on whom Machiavelli modelled *The Prince*, conspired to have his brother murdered. But the Borjas were of Spanish blood, with their family home in the Valencian hill town of Xàtiva (Játiva in *castellano*) and their aristocratic base, bought in the 15th century, in the nearby duchy of Gandía.

Historic Xàtiva

Xàtiva, a pleasant 40-minute drive back from the coast, is the more interesting of the two towns. Try to visit it on Tuesday or Thursday when you can see the market that has existed since medieval times; otherwise, make sure you come when the **museum** is open (Tues–Fri 10am–2pm, 2.30pm in summer, and 4–6pm, Sat 10am–2pm). Its small but interesting collection traces the town's growth from Roman *castrum* (fortress), Visigothic bishopric and cultivated Arab town – thought to be one of the first places where paper was made in Europe – to royal city from the 14th to the 17th centuries. The collection includes a unique Romanesque font, and paintings by José Ribera (d.1591), nicknamed El Spagnaletto, yet another famous native son who made his name in Italy – his paintings are nonetheless considered part of the Spanish School because they had such a great influence.

To make sure you catch everything of interest in the old town, follow the tourist office's numbered walking route, which takes you past old palaces, noble houses – including Alexander VI's birthplace – fountains and churches to **La Seo**, the huge collegiate church, which was sacked in the Civil War (Mon–Sat 10.30am–1pm, closes at noon in summer). On the top of the hill above are the **ruins** (Tues–Fri 10am–7pm, Sat & Sun 10am–8pm, closes one hour earlier in winter; allow an hour) of the Roman to medieval city and castle, destroyed by Philip III in revenge for Xàtiva's siding against him in the War of Succession, and, just below that, the 13th-century church of **San Félix** (open 10am–1pm, 4–7pm or 3–6pm in winter), its doorway built with columns from the Roman Temple on the same site. For lunch, *see page 76*.

Palace of the Borjas

Gandía cannot compare with Xàtiva for atmosphere or monumental wealth, but it does have the **collegiate church** built in the time of of Calixtus III (open for evening Mass) and the sumptuous 16th- to 18th-century former palace of the Borjas, the **Palacio de Santo Duque** (Mon–Fri, guided tours 11am and 6pm; 11 am and 5pm in winter), which is too rich for some tastes. It was turned into Spain's first Jesuit college by the fourth duke, Francisco Borja. Abandoning his ancestors' examples, he turned his back on earthly wealth after the death of his wife, joined the Jesuits and became the Superior of the order. The palace has an outstanding allegorical tiled floor. Nearby is a good cake-shop, **Dolços Toni**, Calle Pares Jesuits 5, where you can recover from so much religiosity.

Right: outside the San Félix church in Xàtiva

7. A NIGHT ON THE TOWN: BENIDORM
AND TERRA MÍTICA *(see map opposite)*

You'll need your own car or a taxi to get from the old town to the clubs off Levante beach. In summer, you can take a ride on the coastal night train, the Trensnochador, which runs from 9pm–5am and stops at Terra Mítica, Europe's largest theme park. Buses run there from Benidorm.

It is easy to knock **Benidorm** – particularly when you have never set eyes on the place. Most people who have actually been there will admit that, even if you don't like package tourism, there is a fascination in the style with which Benidorm, like Las Vegas, does it. One of the largest resorts in the world, a huge fun factory dominated by the 52-storey Hotel Bali – it must be seen to be believed. And, quite apart from all this, its nightlife has something to offer everyone, from a bosanova or garage fan to an 80-year-old granny.

Arrive at sundown as the three miles of white sand are emptying, and you will be in time to catch the evening *paseo*. Follow the signs through the mini-skyscrapers to the **Playa** (or **Platja**) **de Levante** (if you are in a car, leave it in the underground park off Avda de L'Aigüera) and stroll along the front, past the tea cafés where senior citizens happily tango away winter afternoons (many a second romance is formed here). Despite all the foreigners, the *paseo* is also a wonderful cross-section of old and new Spain: mini-skirted girls twice the height of their grandmothers, old men in their berets, women gesticulating with their fans.

The broad expanse of white sand, around which Benidorm grew from a tiny fishing village to a giant resort in only fifty years, are an object lesson in how beaches can be kept clean if you really try. An army of rubbish collectors move in at dusk, and after midnight dumper trucks start the long job of sifting out cigarette butts and oxygenating the sand. Out in the bay, a filter cleans and monitors the water. Beach bars are banned. Hence, despite the 45,000 people who squeeze onto the twin beaches at the height of the season, the sands have been declared among the cleanest in the world.

Once it is dark, walk back to **L'Aigüera** park (dawn–10pm; July–Sept to 1am), designed by controversial Catalan architect Ricardo Bofill. Among the various schemes to move Benidorm up-market, this is the most spectacular and imaginative, and it has an added interest as the first major piece

the north

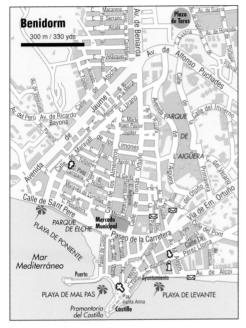

of public architecture in one of the coastal resorts. Built along a dry river valley, its central avenue runs up through sweeping classical perspectives which are transformed at night by blue and white neon lighting. The new town hall in front of the park – also designed by Bofill – is a grandiose testament to the profits of tourism.

Eating options also break the mould, especially now that so many Spanish are coming here. For addresses, see *page 75* – or pick up a snack in the old town. There are a good range of tapas bars on C. Santo Domingo.

Theme parks and Nightclubs

Alternatively, if you've decided on a trip to **Terra Mítica** (opens at 10am all year round; closing times vary betwen 6pm and midnight. Adults 4,600 Ptas, children under 12 and OAPs 3,300 Ptas; reduced prices in winter), Europe's largest theme park covering 105 hectares, you can eat in one of the 80 restaurants there. The park – 3km (2 miles) inland from Benidorm – takes the Mediterranean classical civilisations as its theme; rides include the Magnus Colossus, the largest wooden rollercoaster in Europe. Critics says the technology cannot compare to Port Aventura, the theme park at Salou on the Costa Dorada, but few children are going to notice the difference and the food and shops gain enormously by turning their back on Americana as decisively as the rides.

Back in Benidorm itself are two main centres of nightlife. The first is the old town, where you will find a more native atmosphere in local bars, ice cream parlours and *horchaterías* as well as the gay clubs, recognised by music and lights behind plain façades. As everywhere in Spain, these usually have a relaxed mixed clientele. The other main area is new Benidorm, further towards the edge of town on the Avenida de la Comunitat Valenciano at the far end of the **Levante beach**, where **Penélope** – the biggest disco – and its rivals are clustered together. More interesting in this zone are **L'Anouer** or **Ku**, the ultimate discotheque, or **Conuco**, a lively salsa joint on Avenida Europa where you can also take classes *(see page 79)*.

If you can stick the pace and make it right through the night, then finish off with an early morning cup of hot chocolate at **Buana**, or one of the other bars along the main road in **Villajoyosa** (**La Vila Joiosa**).

Left: Benidorm was a small fishing village only 50 years ago

The Centre
Alicante

8. ALICANTE CITY *(see map, p37)*

A full day exploring Alicante on foot: the castle, museum and old town in the morning; a beach in the afternoon; the small museum of 20th-century art in the early evening.

Alicante (Alacant) is by no means only a tourist centre. Where the beaches end, a Mediterranean city with a life of its own begins. Less culturally dynamic than Barcelona, less historic than Tarragona and less buzzy than Valencia it may be, but it has a good dose of all their qualities and on a far more accessible scale. The best way to get your bearings is to take the clanking lift up from the Paseo Gomez to the **Castillo Santa Bàrbara** (summer 10am–8pm, winter 9am–7pm; park on the opposite side of the road).

Today, after centuries of refortifying and bombardment, the castle is more impressive from below than from inside, but it is worth the trip up to the top for the urban panorama below. Immediately to the south lies the heart of the city, its broad Rambla neatly dissecting the scrambled old town from the more spacious 19th-century grid of streets and shady plazas while, to the north, a great arc of hotel and apartment skyscrapers curves round from the industrial port and a marina to a sweep of white beaches.

City Origins

It is right in the middle of the tourist suburbs, close to Albufereta beach, that the first Alicante grew up. The Greeks gave the Iberian settlement the name Akra Leuke (white peak), from which came the Roman name of Lucentum and the Arab or *valenciano* name of Alacant. The Carthaginians used it as a port, and Hannibal is said to have unloaded his war elephants here. In the late 1990s, after years of excavation, the site of the ancient settlement was opened to the public under the name **Tossal de Manises** (Albufereta; June–Sept Tues–Sun 9am–noon, 6–9pm; Oct–May 9am–1pm, 4–6pm), the hump under which it was hidden for centuries.

Before visiting the site it is worth seeing the spectacular new **Museo Arqueologico de Alicante**, MARQ, (Antiguo Hospital Provincial San Juan de Dios, Pza Dr Gómez Ulla s/n; Tues–Sat 10am–2pm, 4–8pm, Sun and holidays 10am–2pm) behind the castle. Here you can take in the background to prehistoric, Roman, Muslim and medieval Alicante in splendidly atmospheric visual displays with evocative soundtracks and

Left: Alicante has a good selection of beaches
Right: the historic castle is well worth a visit

press-button screens, and you can buy a combined ticket to Lucentum.

The stroll back towards the old town through the small shopping street running around the wonderful, newly restored modernist central market takes you past small shops selling everything from *paella* pans to traditional *alpargatas* or cut-price shoes sold direct from the factory. Walk past the 19th-century theatre – which is worth a peek inside – down the busy Rambla and across into **Calle San Isidro** to arrive at **San Nicolás** (daily, winter: 7.30am–1pm, 5.30–8pm; summer: 7.30am–noon, 6–8.30pm), the town's 17th-century cathedral. It is quite modest in scale and ornament by the standards of Spanish baroque because it was built as a collegiate church. Inside, do not miss the earlier Gothic cloister where a fountain trickles among the ornamental oranges.

A stone's throw beyond is the 18th-century *ayuntamiento* housed in the old **Casa Consistorial** (Mon–Fri 9am–2pm, Sat 9am–1pm), with stunning reliefs both back and front by Juan Batista Borja, who also carved the cathedral door. The first step is used as sea level for all altitude measurements made in Spain. The plaza's finest moment comes every July, on the last night of the *hogueras*, the city's biggest fiesta, when the mayor lights a trapeze-like fuse which sputters over the heads of the assembled crowd towards an enormous wooden sculpture in the middle of the square. As it bursts into flame, the crowd erupts and the **Nit del Foc**, when nearly 100 such bonfires burn in sequence through the city, has officially begun.

Lunch Options

All around the arcaded plaza and dotted around the old town are bars and restaurants that offer a *menú del día* (menu of the day). **Nou Manolín** – which is close to the bullring, a 10-minute walk away – is a cut above the rest, with an excellent wine cellar. It is worth the extra distance if you want to linger over a good meal. For a quick snack on the seafront there are plenty of different options in the mall developments at either end of the harbour. After lunch, **Playa del Postiguet** is a good spot for sunbathing out of season, but when the crowds thicken you may prefer to drive past San Juan to **Cabo de las Huertas**, a rocky oasis about 20 minutes away.

Above: Santa María church
Right: Museo de la Asegurada

Return to the old town, walking up the pedestrianised **Calle Mayor** – the city's main shopping street until the 19th century and still bustling – to explore the **Barrio Santa Cruz**, originally the Muslim part of town and now the most atmospheric in a rakishly down-at-heel way. Doves flutter around the gargoyle and cherub-laden façade of **Santa María** church, built over the main mosque. The church opens for evening Mass at about 6.

A short walk further back and up towards the castle you can visit the **Pozos de Garrigós** (Plaza del Puente s/n; Tues–Fri 10am–2pm, 5–8pm; winter: 4.30–7.30pm; Sat 10am–2pm), four giant urn-like water cisterns built underground by the Muslims to catch the water as it poured down the mountain after heavy rainfall. Closed after the Christian conquest and only rediscovered in 1861, the cisterns are an ingenious piece of engineering and have small changing exhibitions inside. Close by, you can also visit the **Museo de Belenes**.

International Modernism

Next door is the **Museo de la Asegurada** (Pl. de Santa María; Tues–Sat; June–Sept: 10am–1pm, 5–9pm; Oct–May 10am–2pm, 4–8pm, Sun, holidays 10.30am–2.30pm), an excellent contemporary art collection left to the city by the abstract painter Eusebio Sempere. The works track international modernism from Kandinsky to Christo, and represent all the great Spanish names of the 20th century. A major new **Galería Provincial de Bellas Artes** is also due to open in the next few years in the restored Palacio Granna.

Behind the church and museum, small whitewashed houses noisy with early-evening gossip and children's street games wind along and around the base of the castle's mound. In the **Calle San Raphael** there are several small café-bars where you can muster your strength before joining the evening *paseo* along the seafront Explanada. This is a quite different world from

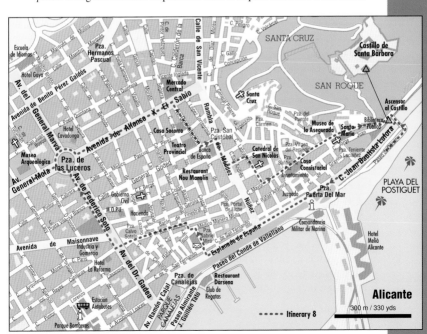

the Barrio de Santa Cruz, a few hundred metres away. Stop off on the way at **Peret's** legendary seafront kiosk to grab a *horchata* (tiger-nut milk), a refreshing drink in which locals like to dunk slabs of almond cake and sponge fingers. Wander under the shade of the huge fig trees, past the municipal bandstand and parents bouncing children on their knees, to the modernist fish market now restored as an exhibition centre. Back at the other end of the harbour, on the Muelle de Levante, is **Dársena**, in the port's new commercial complex, where you can sample 50 types of rice while looking over the harbour *(see page 75)*.

The nightlife in Alicante is never dull. Depending on your tastes there is plenty of action in the bars of the Barrio Santa Cruz or the discos of San Juan *(see page 78)*, and in July and August the Trensnochador train will take you to all the nightspots north to Dénia *(see page 92)*. Alternatively you can hop over from there to Ibiza on the hydrofoil in just a few hours and get lost in Europe's biggest club scene.

9. CRAFT TRADITIONS: NOUGAT AND POTTERY IN JIJONA AND AGOST   *(see map, p46–47)*

From Alicante visit traditional diverse factories and workshops; you should allow four hours for this itinerary.

Many of Alicante's industries, including shoes, toys, textiles, paper, rugs, ceramics and confectionery, have their roots in traditional crafts. Two of the best examples are *turrón*-making in **Jijona** (Xixona) and the potteries and industrial ceramics factories of **Agost**, which have preserved their artisan

roots and small-scale family ownership. Jijona, which is half an hour's drive from Alicante on the road to Alcoi, is the home of Spanish *turrón*, a rich honey-and-almond nougat, which comes either soft and sticky like an oily *halva*, hard and white like French Montelimar, or caramelised and glistening around whole almonds (known as Jijona, Alicante and *guirlache* respectively). Most of the 50 million kilos of *turrón* that is eaten in Spain every Christmas is made here, in small family factories that operate on a semi-artisan basis, the almonds sorted by hand, the traditions passed down the generations. Job contracts are seasonal, for the winter only, and the workers usually move elsewhere for the summer, often running ice cream parlours.

One of the factories, **Turrones El Lobo** (Calle Alcoi 62; Mon–Fri 10am–3.30pm, 4–7pm; Sat morning), organises half-hour visits round the work floor and its private museum, with old manual pestles and mortars, primitive curved-stone rolling boards and wood-fired crucibles turned by donkeys. The shop has every conceivable kind of *turrón* to take home – be realistic and bear in mind the state of your teeth when you make your choice.

Family Potteries

The road to Agost, which has been a pottery town since Roman times, winds up and down over the arid white Sierra de Maigmó and past the **Tibi dam** (*see page 43*). Artisan production here has adapted to the times: the town now survives due to its factories' new direction – the manufacture of industrial ceramics and roof tiles. But it still preserves half a dozen or so of the family potteries, usually inherited through some eight or 10 generations, which continue to manufacture the old-fashioned, unglazed *botijos*, or earthenware water bottles, that cool the water they contain by a process of evaporation. To work well, they have to be made from the right kind of clay (which is found around Agost) and wood-fired in a brick kiln.

Unfortunately, the traditional *botijos* are slowly losing their place to more modern industries. Some of the potters have survived by adapting to the world of today. **Emili Boix**, for example, representing the eighth generation to work in the family pottery concern, tends to create mainly decorative ceramics – some painted in the classical Iberian style. Other potters, such as **Evaristo Viledo** and **Pedro Molla**, Boix's neighbours, stick largely to the production of traditional functional pieces (both potteries are easily found on the main road where it winds out of the top of the town).

Before buying any items that take your fancy here, a visit to the nearby **Museo de Alfarería** (Tues–Sun, summer: 11am–2pm, 5–8pm; winter: 11am–2pm; tel: 96 569 1199) is definitely worthwhile, and will undoubtedly further your appreciation of pottery. The museum's excellent displays on the history of the potteries illustrate the different forms and techniques used. If the owner of the museum has time, she might well be persuaded to show you the chapel of **Santas Justa e Rufina**, patron saints of potters, in the **Calle de Alfarería** – the inside is decorated with wonderful small figures that

Above left: Alicante's seafront Explanada. **Left:** making *turrón* in Jijona
Above: potter with traditional *botijos* in Agost

were made at the time the chapel was built in the 1820s. From the chapel it is only a short walk up to the honey-coloured old town, where you will find plenty of bars for snacks or a refreshing drink.

If you would like to extend the trip and its theme into a full day, you could stay and have lunch in Jijona, which is known especially for *giraboix* – a warming double dish of a broth thickened with egg yolks and a stew consisting of potatoes, white beans and salt-cod – and take in a visit to **Monóvar**'s arts and crafts museum *(see page 45)*.

10. Villena and Elche: Buried History
(see map, p46–47)

A visit to the Iberian gold collection at Villena; in the afternoon a 45-minute drive to the Iberian–Roman site outside Elche, plus Europe's largest palm forest in the town centre.

At a first glance, **Villena** and **Elche** – or Elx in *valenciano* – have little in common: Villena is a bustling small town in the Vinalopó valley, known for the silhouette of its medieval castle and for the strength of its wine; Elche is a dusty city, associated with its date palm forest, mystery play and mushrooming shoe factories. Under the surface though – quite literally –

the two share buried treasures, brought to light towards the end of the 19th century. It was in 1897 that some farm workers inadvertently stumbled upon the *Dama de Elche*, the sculpture that has since become a symbol of the sophistication of Iberian culture. Unfortunately for Elche, the Dama, serenely enigmatic, made her way via dealers to Paris and then back to Madrid, where she maintains pride of place in the Museo Arqueológico. (The authorities have made it quite clear that she will not be returned to her place of origin). Since then, however, many more riches have turned up on the same Iberian and Roman site, where the river city of Illici stood. These Elche has managed to keep.

An Iberian Treasure Trove

A trip to **Villena** transports you even further back into the prehistoric past – another 50,000 or so years. Start the day here in the lovely 17th-century *ayuntamiento*, where the **Museo Arqueológico** (Pl. Santiago 1; Tues–Fri 10am–2pm, 5–8pm; holidays, weekends 11am–1.30pm; call ahead, tel 96 580 1150) is squeezed into one room. This extraordinary museum represents the life's work of one man, José María Soler, who died in 1996. Undoubtedly the star attraction is an incredible Iberian treasure-trove that consists of 30 pieces of solid fluvial gold – bowls and small pots moulded and beaten to look like sea urchins, stunningly beautiful necklaces, bracelets weighing up to half a kilo (1 lb) each and giant earstuds. Soler found these priceless

Above: José María Soler with one of his finds. **Above right:** Villena's old-world charm
Right: Villena is dominated by its medieval castle

items in the course of one weekend in the mid-1960s when he was working as a civil servant for the post office. Researchers believe the relatively advanced metal-working techniques, for example the methods of drilling, come from the Tartessan civilisation.

The rest of the collection, which often gets overlooked, comes from a large number of nearby sites, one of them the Bronze Age capital of Cabeza Redonda – where the treasure was found – and another, called the Casa de Lara, which is unique in that it straddles 8,000 years of history and technological development. Other gems include a second (smaller) gold 'treasure', a unique clay crucible, a drinking bottle with a double mouth – perhaps for *anís* and water, and finds of craftwork made from *esparto* grass and rush from a new site at Terlinques.

A Controversial Font

While in Villena, visit the 15th- and 16th-century church of **Santiago**, one of the finest examples of Levantine Gothic architecture in Alicante province: its fluted cable columns, topped by lovely floral capitals, soar on up into high, shadowy vaulting, and next to the altar is a wonderful, richly carved font, also 16th-century, by sculptor Jacopo Florentino, one of Michelangelo's assistants, who moved to Spain and settled in Villena. (The font spent many years in a backroom because the priest objected to the bared breasts displayed around the outside.) You can also climb, past the rich baroque façade of the **Iglesia de Santa María**, to the severe castle *(see page 49)*.

Elche

The quickest route to Elche is via the motorway to Alicante. It is then only a short drive to the **Museo Monogràfico de L'Alcúdia** (Tues–Sat; Oct–Mar: 10am–5pm; Apr–Sept: 10am–2pm, 4–8pm, Sun 10am–2pm; small entrance fee), on the site of **Illici**, one of the country's most important Iberian sites. Be warned that it is badly signposted in town – follow signs to Dolores and watch for the turnoff at 2.2km). The museum is a labour of love, this time by the Ramos family, which owns the farm and which has produced three

generations of archaeologists. Astonishingly, given the value of the site, only one tenth of it has so far been excavated, although the family organises digs every summer. The 3,000 pieces on show and the highlights of the site itself deserve at least an hour of the visitor's time.

Back in the dusty city centre, housed in the east wing of the **Alcázar** or **Palacio de Altamira** (Tues–Fri 10.30am–1.30pm, 5–9pm; weekends, holidays 10am–1pm) is the town's answer to the Museo Arqueológico, where prize pieces from Alcudia are on show. Check out the pair of prowling sphinxes and a headless Roman Venus. The Palacio's walls and towers are also open. From here it is but a short walk to the other monuments in the centre: the Muslim **Calaforra**, or watchtower, with its *mudéjar* hallway and, just beyond, the 16th-century façade of the **Convento de la Mercè**.

The Last Mystery Play

Behind the Convento are the well-restored **Baños Arabes** (Muslim baths; Tues–Sat 10.30am–1.30pm, 5–9pm, Sun 10am–1pm); the *ayuntamiento*, with its 14th-century clock striking on the quarter hour; and the overwhelming baroque **Basílica** (daily 7am–1.30pm, 5.30–9pm). Here, the spectacular **Misterio de Elche**, the only mystery play still performed in a Catholic church, takes place every August. The play tells of the Assumption of the Virgin Mary in a sung drama. It is the only European mystery play that has kept its medieval form (a 14th-century text) and is still performed by townspeople in a church designed around the play: in the course of the performance, spectacular aerial machinery is lowered to the floor of the church from the dome. Book tickets well in advance from the Elche tourist office. The final *Nit de l'Alba* features a stunning, explosive fireworks display.

The glorious small monastery church of **San José**, a 15-minute walk away on the far side of the river, is well worth the effort for its refreshingly humble Franciscan version of baroque, with original frescoes, *azulejos* and woodcarving. You can stroll there and back over La Pasarela and through the former Muslim quarter, or Raval, marked out by its tightly packed streets. Have a drink at La Glorieta before visiting the **Hort del Cura** (Tues–Sun 9am–6pm, closes at 8.30pm in summer; entrance fee), the botanical garden

in the palm forest. The palm forests have now been added to the UNESCO cultural heritage list. The Hort, laid out in the 19th century, is known for the Imperial Palm, a hermaphrodite palm tree that changed sex after about 70 years of life and sprouted seven new trunks, one of which produces dates. But for many it is the artfulness of the planting between the palms, the contrasts between cactuses and lilies, that makes the garden so seductive.

Tailoring supper to the size of your pocket, you can choose between various restaurants in the centre or on the edge of town *(see page 76)*, where you can try the great local speciality of *arroz con costra*, rice with pork and sausages buried under a golden egg crust.

11. A PICNIC AT TIBI RESERVOIR   *(see map, p46–47)*

An expedition to see one of the oldest working dams in Europe, a 50-minute drive inland from Alicante.

It might seem that the village of **Tibi** has little to make it stand out from countless other villages in the inland sierras of Alicante: it has a few shops and bars, a village cooperative and a shady main street. What makes it worth visiting, however, are its reservoir and dam, built over 14 years at the end of the 16th century (1580–94) to irrigate the Alicante *huerta*, which still function today.

The reservoir and dam are most easily reached off the road from Alicante to Castallá. Coming from Alicante, turn right down an unmarked road into a small housing development known as the **Urbanización Maigmó**, about 100 metres (330ft) after a garage and 200 metres (660ft) before the

Above: Elche's baroque Basílica
Right: the Tibi dam

turn-off to **Agost** (if you get lost, ask at the garage for the *embalse*). Take the second road on the right, which is signposted, and follow it round, then keep straight all the way past four small junctions, until you come to a farm. Here the road swings right and down towards the reservoir until, after a total of 5km (3 miles), it reaches a clearing for parking. Leave the car here.

There is a choice of two approaches to the dam, one a short cut up the slope to your left, which brings you straight out on top of the dam; the alternative option is more spectacular but is not advisable for children or for those without a head for heights. This route heads down a path to the right to a small bridge with a plaque dedicated to Charles IV, from where you get the first complete view of the dam, directly upstream. Built between a narrow gorge, the dam's overall dimensions are nothing like those of many modern dams. But the severe curved wall, making brilliant use of the natural geography, is a magnificent sight when you stand below it, listening to the eerie sound effects of the water and air eddying within. Watch the overflow splash from above, down onto the rocks below.

A dizzying climb of more than 100 steps cut into the rock, with only a crumbling rail to hold, takes you up to the top of the dam. Set into its worn blocks of stone is a plaque commemorating its refurbishment in 1794. This is a wonderful place to have a picnic, looking out onto the reservoir on one side and down the wall of the dam on the other.

12. THE WINE COUNTRY OF MONOVAR
(see map, p46–47)

Monóvar is a 45-minutes drive from Alicante. Allow two hours to visit the town, and another three to explore the surrounding wine villages.

Until the end of the 19th century, Monóvar's red wine was among the most sought-after in Europe. Transparent and slightly sweet, it was said to be an aphrodisiac – probably on account of its high alcohol content. It was also among the most expensive: in the late 19th century, during a golden age that Monóvar enjoyed following the destruction of French vineyards by phylloxera, a single shipload covered the entire building costs of the casino in Monóvar three times over. Tastes in wine changed however, and the

French vineyards were replanted. Today the vineyards of Monóvar are little known. This makes them all the more interesting to visit, since the wines are hard to find outside the region, the villages remain unspoilt and the *bodegas* are not over-commercialised. In summer they are usually open from 9am until 2pm; the rest of the year you can also taste and buy later in the afternoon (4–7pm). From the coast, take the back road from Alicante via **Agost** *(see page 38)* and **Novelda**, which passes first through almond groves and then, after you have crossed under the motorway, into the vineyards. Trellised vines run in an unbroken sea until they rise, banked in hillside terraces, to meet the sierras looming in the background. The native Monastrel grapes are largely used for making red wine; Verdil for white.

A Leaning Clock Tower

Monóvar (Monóver) is only a small town, but it has an interesting personality and a wonderfully jumbled collection of local arts, crafts and work tools. The clock tower leans drunkenly at the top of the town, and the church is missing one of its bell towers. The most fascinating of its many curiosities is the 19th-century pharmacy and shop that are on display at the **Museo de Artes y Oficios** (Calle Salamanca 6; Mon–Fri 10am–2pm, 4–6pm, Sat 11am–2pm, by advance arrangement; tel: 96 547 0270). Monóvar was the birthplace of **Azorín**, prolific essayist, novelist and politician of the late 19th century.

Among the *bodegas*, **Salvador Poveda** (Calle Benjamín Palencia; daily 7am–3pm), the biggest, is right in the centre of town. Salvador Poveda is famous for its fragrant pudding wine, Fondillón, which is apparently King Juan Carlos's favourite after-dinner tipple. Fondillón needs to be matured for 20 years (beware of cheap imitations), but the *bodega* also produces blood-coloured reds and excellent, delicate rosés. Their character comes from the local wine-making method, in which the rosé is fermented from must drawn off during a first light crushing of the grapes; the red is derived from a *doble pasta* in which the first batch of must and grapes is mixed with a second one in the same vat prior to fermentation. Another family *bodega* on the edge of town, **Primitivo Quiles**, produces similar wines and delicious vermouth.

From Monóvar, you can continue on a short circular route which takes you around the **Sierra de Reclot** and through the other wine villages – **Hondón** (where a cooper still works), **Mañar**, **Culebrón**, **Pinoso**, **Algueña** and **La Romana**. All these villages are known for their earthy country cuisine, especially rice with rabbit and snails, and *gazpachos*, which here is a type of game stew. Go easy on the wine, though, especially if you have been tasting – at Culebrón, they say it is strong enough to revive dead men.

Left: the fruit of the fields
Above: refreshments in a local bar

alicante & surrounds

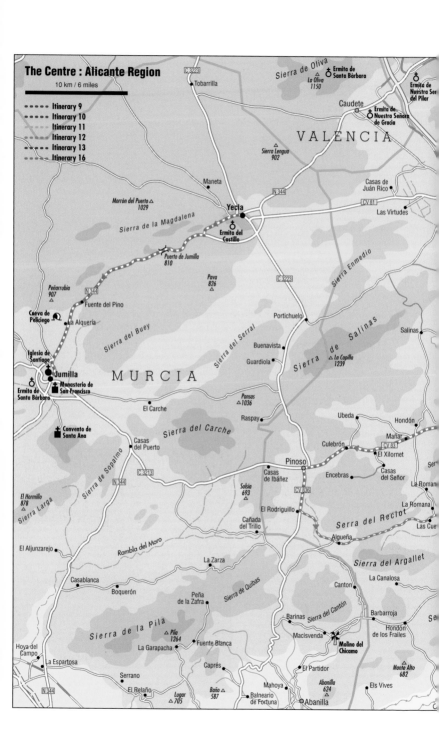

The Centre : Alicante Region

10 km / 6 miles

- Itinerary 9
- Itinerary 10
- Itinerary 11
- Itinerary 12
- Itinerary 13
- Itinerary 16

Sierra de Oliva

Ermita de Santa Bárbara

La Oliva 1150

Ermita de Nuestra Ser del Pilar

Tobarrilla

Caudete

Ermita de Nuestra Señora de Gracia

VALENCIA

Sierra Lengua 902

Maneta

N 344

Casas de Juán Rico

CV 81

Las Virtudes

Morrón del Puerto 1029

Yecla

Ermita del Castillo

Sierra de la Magdalena

Puerto de Jumilla 810

Pava 826

C 3223

Sierra Enmedio

Peñarrubia 907

N 344

Fuente del Pino

Cueva de Peliciego

La Alquería

Portichuelo

Sierra de Salinas

Salinas

Buenavista

La Capilla 1239

Sierra del Buey

Sierra del Serral

Guardiola

Sierra de

Iglesia de Santiago

Jumilla

Monasterio de San Francisco

MURCIA

Pansas 1036

Ubeda

Hondón

Ermita de Santa Bárbara

El Carche

Raspay

Mañar

Culebrón

CV 83

El Xilornet

Convento de Santa Ana

Casas del Puerto

Sierra del Carche

Pinoso

Casas del Señor

Ser

C 3213

Sierra de Sopalmo

N 344

Casas de Ibáñez

Encebras

La Roman

El Hormillo 878

Solsia 693

CV 836

La Romana

Sierra Larga

El Rodriguillo

Serra del Rec!ot

Las Cue

El Aljunzarejo

Cañada del Trillo

Algueña

Rambla del Moro

La Zarza

Sierra del Argallet

Casablanca

Boquerón

Peña de la Zafra

Sierra de Quibas

Canton

La Canalosa

Barbarroja

Barinas

Sierra del Cantón

Hondón de los Frailes

Sierra de la Pila

Pila 1264

Macisvenda

Se

Hoya del Campo

La Garapacha

Fuente Blanca

Molino del Chicamo

La Espartosa

Caprés

El Partidor

Monte Alto 682

Serrano

Mahoya

Abanilla 624

Els Vives

El Relaño

Lugar 705

Baño 587

Balneario de Fortuna

Abanilla

N 344

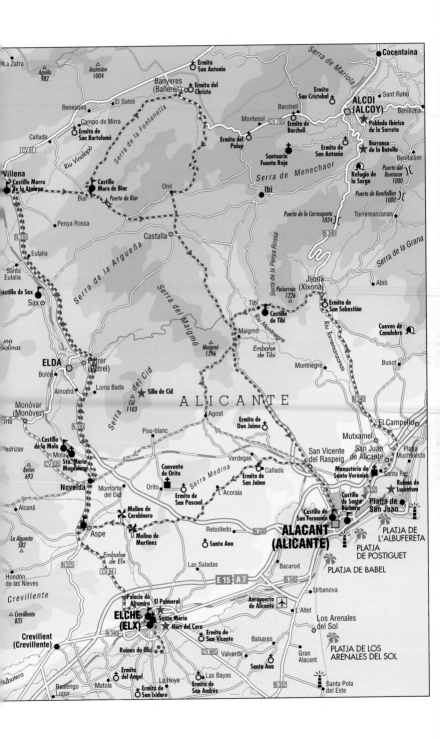

13. FRONTIER TERRITORY: THE VINALOPO VALLEY
(see map, p46–47)

Starting at Alicante, allow a leisurely day to see all of the castles in the Vinalopó region. For a half-day itinerary, turn back at Biar (Bihar).

The broad valley floor of the **Vinalopó** has always been both a strategic route and frontier territory. This is where the cultures of the Bronze Age separated into different forms, the Carthaginians were defeated by the Romans, the Muslim kingdom of Murcia met its northern boundary and Castile battled with Aragon for more than a century. Today, perched on rocky outcrops, medieval castles stand as silent markers of the old Muslim and Christian frontiers. The fortresses preside over almond trees, olive groves and the vineyards from which the valley's famous table grapes originate.

Now that the castles have no military function, it is easy to forget their former importance. As Philip V wrote in 1704, during the War of Spanish Succession, 'It is more important for me to keep Alicante than Valencia, because if Valencia were lost, which God forfend, it alone will be lost; but if Alicante were lost, both Valencia and Castile would be lost.'

An Impregnable Tower

The castle of **Santa Bàrbara** in Alicante, which was a virtually impregnable tower in Muslim times, features many later additions. Among its surviving elements, the most fascinating are the 16th- and 17th-century additions (modelled on the French Vauban system) and the sheer scale of the walled area, which could garrison up to 40,000 men.

From Alicante, take the road through **San Vicente de Raspeig** and **Aspe** to **Novelda** (about 40 minutes drive). Just beyond is the castle of **La Mola**, which is famous for its superb 12th-century triangular tower, designed by Ibrahim of Tunis, a famous Arab military engineer. The tower stands above

Above: Sax's Hispano-Arabic castle

an eye-catching small modernist sanctuary designed by Sala, a disciple of the inimitable Antonio Gaudí. Back in the town you might also want to visit the perfectly preserved **Casa Museo Modernista** (Calle Mayor 22–4; Sun–Thur 9.30am–1.30pm, 4.30–6.30pm, opens 9am Fri, Sat 11am–2pm). It is then a 15-minute drive up the motorway to **Villena**. The journey passes two more Hispano-Arabic castles: **Petrel** and **Sax**. The latter has an extraordinary setting – it is perched like an eagle's nest above the old town (the key is kept in the *ayuntamiento*). Both castles have been much restored.

For this reason, Villena's castle, **La Atalaya** (literally, 'the watchtower'), is more impressive when seen from close up. It is usually left open – just unlatch the studded door. Heavily fortified by the Almohades in the 12th century – their brick vaulting survives inside the superb keep – it became the centre of a powerful feudal state owing allegiance to Castile. The castle controlled, and was in turn protected by, a string of smaller castles: **La Mola**, **Sax**, **Elda** and, in Albacete province on the road to Madrid, **Chinchilla** and **Almansa**. In the 15th century it fell into the hands of the Pachecos, the hugely powerful masters of the Order of Santiago. It was the Pachecos who built the thick double outer walls and the upper watchtowers of the keep. You can walk right around the walls, which took a bad battering in the War of Independence against the French. Below the castle spreads the old town.

Castle Towns

From Villena, you can take either of two routes. The longer option loops north to the town of **Bañeres** (Bañyeres de la Mariola), which has a Gothic church and yet another Hispano-Arabic castle (the key is at Calle Castillo 20; ring in advance to arrange to pick it up; tel: 966-567315 or 966-567756 on Sun). This castle was in Aragonese hands after the Reconquest. It looks out over four provinces – Valencia, Murcia, Albacete and Alicante – and marks part of the border between *castellano*- and *valenciano*-speaking territories.

If you have only a morning or afternoon, you can go straight to **Biar** on

the Aragonese side of the old border. The prettiest of all these castle towns, it has a hilly old quarter that rises sharply as you climb up the long flights of steps to reach the castle. The scene of a hard-fought battle in the Reconquest, it features the oldest surviving example of octagonal Almohade vaulting. Stop in the **Plaça de le Constitució** below for a glance at the church's mix of styles: it has a Renaissance doorway and baroque frescoes over a Gothic form.

The road on to Alicante will also take you past **Castalla**, where there are more castle ruins and a great restaurant *(see page 76)*.

Left: a public fountain in Biar

14. SOUTHERN COSTA BLANCA: ALICANTE TO DEHESA
(see map, p52–53)

The coast road south from Alicante passes Santa Pola, where you can
take a boat to Tabarca island. Further south, past pine forests,
Guardamar is 1¼ hours drive from Alicante.

The road south from Alicante cuts through a flat, luminous landscape past an
open shoreline which at first sight appears to be quite lifeless. Only dusty
palms and apartment blocks seem to break the long stretches of sand. Closer
inspection, however, reveals a wealth of fine features: the fortified island and
marine nature reserve at Santa Pola; a string of salt pans which are now
protected as nature reserves for their birdlife; and some fine unspoilt beaches.

Santa Pola is the most interesting of the southern resorts once you have
made it to the seafront. The most attractive road from the north, reached
through the Gran Alacant estate, runs along Calabessí beach. Next to the port,
home to the largest deep sea and coastal fleet of the Mediterranean, you
can catch a boat to **Tabarca** *(for sailings see page 93)*, the main island of a
small archipelago in the bay, which Charles III fortified and settled with
Genoese prisoners in the 18th century. The walled town now looks like a
grandiose folly, the unfinished church and entrance arch absurdly oversized

next to the squat fishing shacks and
dusty roads. On the other half of the
island you will find the old lighthouse
and solar station that generates the island's electricity. (A walk around the
island takes about 1½ hours.)

A Double Life

The island now has only about 100
residents, who follow a double life
according to the season. In winter they
tend to work on the fishing boats and
in summer, in the *chiringuitos*, or
beach restaurants. Visitors come here for a variety of reasons, some for the
refreshing breeziness of the beaches and the *caldero* in the restaurants, others to do some serious snorkelling or sub-aqua diving in the protected waters
around the island. Ecologists consider the marine reserve that surrounds
the archipelago a model of its type, which it is hoped will be replicated
elsewhere along the shore to regenerate the underwater ecosystem.

You can stay on the island until sunset, when it is at its emptiest and most
beautiful, or return to Santa Pola in time to see the aquarium and clinic for
sick turtles in the **Plaza Francisco Fernández Ordoñez** (Tues–Sun, summer:
11am–1pm, 6–10pm; winter: 10am–1pm, 5–7pm). Afterwards you might
head for one of the busy fish restaurants *(see page 78)*. The most interesting
local dish is the *gazpacho de pescado*, a marine adaptation of the inland
game stews, but all the usual rices and *caldero* are excellent too.

If you decide to continue going south, the beach road south from the town
centre brings you out abruptly at huge white mounds of salt extracted from

Above: return of the fishermen. **Above right:** on Tabarca island
Right: the Santa Pola–Tabarca ferry

the chequered salt-pans that have constituted a natural park since 1994. The park was formed to protect the flamingos, grebes and other migratory birds – some 250 recorded species – that pass through here every spring and autumn. About 20 minutes to the south is the beach of La Marina, backed by pine glades planted on the dunes that run south all the way to **Guardamar de Segura**. The beach is now being overtaken by high-rise tourist blocks, but the pine groves around the mouth of the River Segura have become a park, in the middle of which you can visit a mosque unearthed from a thick blanket of sand. In the town itself are a number of fish restaurants specializing in the local *langostines* which are expensive these days, but the *caldero* is excellent.

Further south, behind the spreading mass of **Torrevieja** – one of Spain's fastest-growing resorts made up largely of holiday flats and homes – are two larger salt lakes covering a total of 2,100 hectares (5,200 acres). They still produce a million tons of salt a year, but are now also a bird reserve (Mon–Fri 8am–3pm, Tues, Thur 4–6pm, weekends 9am–3pm). In the town itself, the salt silos and wharves in the harbour are currently being restored to house the **Museo del Mar y la Sal**; another part of the harbour is used to stage the summer song festival dedicated to the Latin American *habaneras* that were brought back here in the 19th century by emigrants *(see p 85)*. Just down the road, on the Paseo Vista Alegre, is the splendid *fin de siècle* **Casino** where you can sit and watch the locals go about their business over a drink and a snack. For more deserted beaches and a refreshing afternoon swim, drive on to the far end of **Dehesa de Campoamor**, avoiding the splurges of building. Here rust-coloured cliffs drop down to small and often empty coves, and the water is warm enough for swimming well into the autumn.

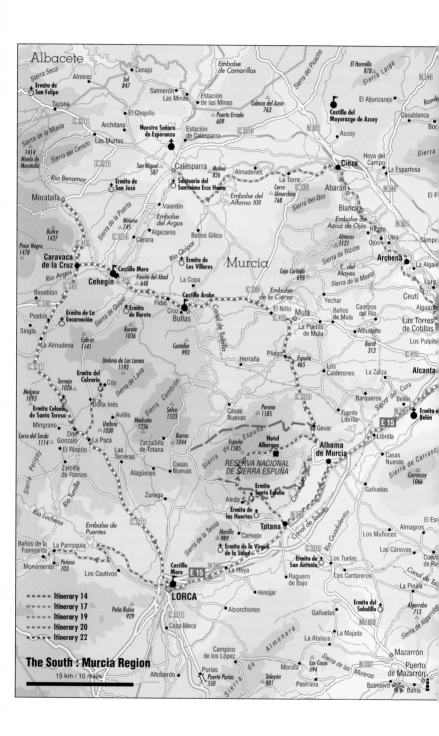

The South : Murcia Region

15 km / 10 miles

- **---** Itinerary 14
- **---** Itinerary 17
- **---** Itinerary 19
- **---** Itinerary 20
- **---** Itinerary 22

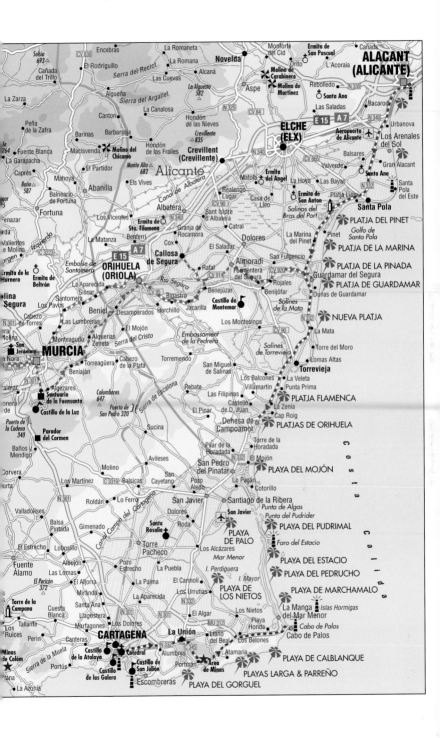

The South
Murcia Region

15. MURCIA CITY: SPANISH BAROQUE *(see map, p56)*

A full day exploring Murcia's unique baroque art and architecture.

Murcia is a wonderfully satisfying tourist city: there's so much to see, and yet all of it is within easy walking distance. In summer the breezeless heat is intense, beating you back off the streets for long rests in cafés or ice-cream-parlours. Ideally, you need to come in spring or autumn and allow several days, so that you can wander at leisure around the shops, parks and museums, and, in the mellow evenings, get under the skin of the southern street life. The best time of all to come is during Holy Week, to see the processions and the explosively colourful spring fiestas which follow close on its heels.

If you have only one day, then concentrate on the city's hoard of baroque art and architecture. It is splendid, it is unique and, even for those who think they don't like baroque, it is fascinating because it captures the spirit of the place. Here, distilled in stone and marble and painted wood, are the exuberance of the fertile *huerta*, the drama of religious fervour, and the love of ornamental detail inherited from the Muslim centuries.

They are all shown in detail in the **Museo de la Ciudad** (Pl. Agustinas 5; Tues–Sat 10am–2pm, 5–8pm, Sun 11am–2pm; weekdays only in summer), which tells the city's story in a lively way with sounds and interactive displays on everything from prehistoric food and Muslim art to the famous Nativity figures made by local potters today.

The **Cathedral** is best approached through the **Plaza Cardinal Belluga** so that your first impression is of the superb main façade. Designed by Valencian architect and sculptor Jaime Bort, it is a perfect balance of ornament and structure, a symbolic gateway to the region, brilliantly adapted to the building and its setting. Other highlights of the Cathedral, which was originally the site of the Great Mosque, are the **Capilla de los Vélez**, its 15th-century white stone stunningly embroidered with detail inside (it is regarded as one of the best examples of Isabelline Gothic architecture) and the cathedral **museum** (10am–1pm, 5–7pm, 8pm in summer).

From here, take a quick look at the crumbling **bishop's palace** and the lovely oval **Iglesia de San Juan de Dios**, restored in 1996, then cross the river to the **Plaza de Camachos** (intended to be oval), where the city's bullfights were held. Both this and the **Puente Viejo**, with its curious shrine at one end, were worked on by Bort as part of the remodelling of the city centre. The motifs of his work – the broken arched cornice, the allegorical figures, the decorated columns – are echoed in buildings elsewhere in the city.

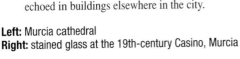

Left: Murcia cathedral
Right: stained glass at the 19th-century Casino, Murcia

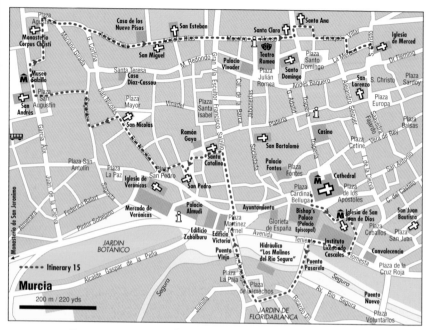

Murcia

Baroque Masterclass

The essence of Murcian baroque can be seen in the work of Francisco Salzillo (1707–83), the sculptor whose life-size processional figures and altarpieces adorn so many of the churches around the region. The realism Salzillo added to these idealised figures, capturing them in mid gesture as if with the camera shutter, gives them a heightened dramatic quality and extraordinary emotional power. In part that skill was inherited from his father, a Neapolitan sculptor. In the **Museo Salzillo** (Pl. de San Augustín 3; Tues–Sat 9.30am–1pm, 3–6pm, 4–7pm in summer; Sun and holidays 11am–1pm; July and Aug weekdays only) devoted to his work are nine massive *pasos*, processional groups that he carved between 1752 and 1778, and a collection of his nativity figures which reflect the same narrative qualities together with a closely observed realism.

On the way to the museum through the old town, you pass three churches – **San Pedro**, **Santa Catalina**, **San Nicolás** – and just beyond are another trio – **San Miguel**, **Santa Ana** and **Santa Clara** – all with fine façades and more Salzillos. Most are open for evening Mass every day, on Saturday afternoons and all day on Sundays. The **Iglesia de Merced** is also outstanding. There are plenty of bars and cafés en route for coffee and *aperitivos*.

Back in town, the baroque spirit was reincarnated in modernist form at the end of the 19th century. Among the examples scattered around the city, the **Casino**, on Calle Trapería, decorated in the 1890s, is unmissable, with its wildly extravagant Arab and Pompeiian patios, and the plushest 'ladies' cloakroom' in town (open all day). The **Casa de Andrés Almansa** also has an interesting modernist façade. They are both in the main shopping and bar area, which are a hive of activity in early evening.

A final interesting visit is the **Museo Ramón Gaya** (Pl. Santa Catalina; Tues–Sat 10am–2pm, 5–8pm, Sun 11am–2pm; weekdays only in summer) dedicated to the painter who, like so many of his generation, has spent most of his life in political exile.

16. THE MURCIAN WINE COUNTRY: JUMILLA, YECLA AND BULLAS *(see map, p46–47)*

Allow 1 hour to reach Yecla from Alicante or 1¼ from Murcia city and 20 minutes on to Jumilla, where there is a good restaurant for lunch. Bullas' hilly vineyards lie 45 minutes drive west of Murcia city.

Where **Murcia** bulges north towards **La Mancha** and opens up into gentle sierras and plateaux, the landscape becomes reminiscent of the *meseta* of nearby Castile. The horizons, wide and full of light, are sparsely populated and cut across by straight roads; the farming land is planted with wheat, olives and vines. Of the three, it is the vines which dominate today. **Yecla** is the largest of the region's three up-and-coming wine *denominaciones*. 'This good town of countrymen…' wrote the novelist Azorín in the early 20th century, 'they love, but love the earth…and they have enormous faith, the faith of the early mystics…this is the old Spain, legendary, heroic.'

The legacy of the faith is a string of churches. Cutting up towards the old town along Calle Perales and San Francisco, you will pass three of them along the way: **San Roque** (with a wonderful *mudéjar* wooden ceiling), **San Francisco** (Renaissance to baroque) and, further up, the massive blue-domed **Iglesia de la Purísima**, which the town struggled and scraped to build for a whole century (*c*1750–1868). At the very top, on the **Plaza Mayor**, stand the mellow-stoned Renaissance **granary** and 19th-century **corn exchange**, and the Church of **San Salvador**, badly damaged but with its 16th-century pyramidal tower intact (in particular, check out the carved frieze of faces under the parapet).

The agricultural base of the town has disappeared now, replaced by furniture manufacturing which grew out of coopering. But the native Monastrell vines remain all-important. On the edge of town, at the massive **Cooperativa de la Purísima**, one of the largest in Spain, you can taste and buy the local reds, which vary between powerful table wines in the old style, with a lot of body and colour – sometimes called macho wines – and smoother, fruity blends adapted to modern drinking tastes, for which the harvest is brought forward to reduce the sugar content of the grapes.

The reds from the neighbouring **Jumilla** region, a 20-minute drive from Yecla, have been famed since

Left: a view of Jumilla

Roman times. They are even more full-bodied (some are 16° strong), a result of intense summer heat and the age of the vines, which are the only Spanish and among the very few European vines not to have been damaged by phylloxera. On the way into town, at **La Alquería**, you will pass the co-operative of **San Isidro**, the town's largest *bodega*, which sells table wine from

the barrel, bottled vintages matured in oak (1973, 1980 and 1981 are prime years), *vino rancio* matured in wood, sweet *mistela* and delicious local cheeses resembling mild young Manchegos. For those who are interested, Jumilla also has a small wine museum (Calle Garcia Lorca 1; tel: 968 756 064 to arrange visits).

Jumilla is, quite apart from the fame of its wines, a charming small market town. It boasts the 16th-century monastery of **Santa Ana** (with an eccentric museum of curiosities brought by Franciscans from all over the world), a private house designed by Gaudí, and **Casa Sebastián** – a wonderful market restaurant with crates of provisions stacked around the walls, hatches opening into the small kitchen and no written menu. But the lack of fuss is deceptive. Fina and Sebastián Bernal have decades of experience and it shows. Eat, drink from the ample cellar and enjoy *(see page 76)*.

Further south, in the hills west of Murcia city, is **Bullas**, the smallest of the region's denominations, where a cooler, wetter climate gives the wines a more restrained character. Here a small specialist company will organise tastings and trips to the vineyards or *bodegas* (Mundo Enológico; tel: 968 654 205).

17. DOWN THE SEGURA VALLEY: CALASPARRA TO MURCIA CITY *(see map, p52–53)*

The drive down the dramatically beautiful Segura Valley to Murcia city can be completed in 2 hours but is more enjoyable taken slowly over the course of the day: you can also continue through the flatter lower valley past historic Orihuela to an unusual Mediterranean garden at Jacarilla.

Following rivers is one of the best ways of exploring Spain. The **Segura** is no exception. Rising high in the sierras of Jaen, it slows to a glassy snake by the time it reaches Murcia city. But behind that deceptive quietness it is an immensely powerful river, irrigating a lush swathe of fruit orchards and citrus groves that cut through the dry sierras and plains, villages and towns, narrowing and widening around the river as it runs down to the coastal plain.

Join the river at **Calasparra**, famous for its rice fields ever since the time of Philip V. At this

Above: quenching thirst, local style
Left: citrus groves at Ojós

point the water is very clean, rushing through the spectacular **Cañón de los Almudenes**, which is signposted off the road along the left bank to Cieza. There is a place to swim here, but be careful, however: below the dam the water is extremely dangerous. You can also take a boat trip down the canyon (tel: 968 723 000).

For the drive down to **Cieza**, double back to Calasparra and take the picturesque road along the right bank, passing a reservoir and pine forests before dropping down to the river and the lush *huerta* for the first time. Just before Cieza is the impressive Atalaya, with panoramic views, where the Muslim citadel of Sisáya was built into the rock. New archaeological excavations are revealing extraordinarily well-preserved houses currently on view as life-size models in the small museum in the town centre. The museum also has displays on local cave paintings.

A Land of Plenty

Follow the signs out of town for Blanca and Abarán. Here the valley suddenly narrows into the dramatically beautiful valley of **Ricote**, the road dipping and curving past plum and peach orchards, with the silhouette of Cieza castle perched above. These orchards are largely new, planted since the small dam at Ojós allowed irrigation some 12 years ago. But the citrus groves further down, at **Blanca** and **Ojós**, standing out against the mountainsides like an oasis in the desert, recreate a sense of Muslim Spain. This is not merely poetic licence. The Muslims first started irrigating the area in the 8th century, and they stayed here until 1611. Their imprint is all around you in the walled paths running between the groves and in the occasional water wheels at the side of the river. Many of these have now been replaced by electric pumps, but one of the largest working wheels in Europe, over 11 metres (36 feet) in diameter, is still in operation at Alberán as are another half dozen wheels along the river. A boat trip in this part of the valley can be organised from Blanca (tel: 968 778 124).

The **Vega Alta** – or upper river plain – ends in style at **Archena**, where 19th-century hotels stand over the thermal baths just outside town. Both the swimming pool in the sub-tropical gardens – you pay at the office – and the bar give a wonderful taste of *belle époque* elegance.

The road runs from here towards the small group of villages in the original Murcian *huerta*, or market garden, which was planted by the Romans and then extended by the Arabs. Since the middle of the 19th century it has

Above: water wheel at La Ñora

steadily expanded, and now produces more lemons than any other region in Europe – as well as oranges, peppers, garlic and three crops a year of other vegetables and fruit. Inevitably, preserving factories soon moved in – their 19th-century chimneys still break the skyline at **Molina de Segura** – and today, with the size of the *huerta* doubling again in the last 10 years, straggling agribusiness calls the tune. The river itself has coped, but only at the cost of pollution and falling water levels.

Nonetheless, there are interesting reminders of past times: at **Javalí Nuevo**, the small 10th-century *contraparada*, which still stands in the river, and, at **Alcantarilla**, another *noria* or Arab water wheel, which has a dou-

ble system of 'live' and 'dead' water, taking it from the river and putting it back in again. It stands in the garden of the **Museo Etnológico de la Huerta** (Ctra de Alcantarilla, by Alcantarilla turning; look for the water wheel on your right; Tues–Fri 10am–7.30pm, 10.30am–6pm in winter; weekends 10.30am–1.30pm, 10.30am–1pm and 3–5.30pm in winter). The displays of tools, costumes, ceramics, woodcarving and the reconstructed *barraca*, or cane and adobe cottage, describe a way of life that has now largely disappeared. All that remains today are a few words of the local dialect, *panocho*, the dances and songs of the spring fiestas, and the cuisine and the crafts that have now found a new lease of life.

It is a short drive from here into **Murcia city**, originally built in the 9th century as an ideal place to bridge the river. After crossing over the **Puente Viejo**, you can park and stroll along the river bank, taking in the **Cathedral** and the hydraulics museum in the converted **mill** (Plaza de los Molinos, Mon–Sat 11am–2pm, 5–8pm; July and Aug Mon–Fri 10am–2pm, 5–8pm) just below the bridge. For full details of the city, *see page 55*.

The Lower Valley

From the centre of Murcia city, drive south along the road marked for the **Santuario de Fuensanta**, then turn to follow the right bank of the river, invisible behind rustling fields of sweet corn, sugar-cane, cotton and newer tropical fruits or flowers. From **Alquerías** to **Beniel**, you can follow a small farm road between the orchards. If you drive up to the sanctuary at **Orihuela** there is a wonderful view over the sea of mottled greens on the valley floor. Orihuela's old centre *(described in more detail on page 62)* repays leisurely exploration. Take the road down the right bank to Bigastro and **Jacarilla**, where there is a lovely garden laid out around the country house of the **Marqueses de Fontalbán** (9am–1pm, 5–6pm; access the garden via the children's playground at other times).

Above: selling fish at Guardarmar

18. A Morning at the Spa: Mula and Archena
(see map, p52–53)

Allow 1 hour by car from Alicante, or 45 minutes from Murcia. The spa is only open in the morning.

Murcia region is something of a paradise for lovers of spa towns, with a choice of nearly half a dozen thermal baths dotted around the countryside. Most have been in continual use since at least Roman times, and remain wonderfully old-fashioned in different ways. This is especially true of two small spas in the Sierra de Espuña: **Fuensanta**, tucked away an hour's drive from Lorca up a small road into the sierras and completely uncommercialised (the waters are recommended for skin treatment); and the baths in the middle of the small town of **Alhama de Murcia** (next to the Parque Cubana; open Mon–Sat 9am–1pm, 4–7pm), which are pleasantly casual and recently restored. Two other spas closer to Murcia city offer very different experiences. **Baños de Mula** is a wonderful spa village nestling in the Mula Valley. Here you can rent rooms or flats with private mineral baths inside them for 8–10,000 Ptas. It is also possible to bathe in a communal source and to have hydromassage. The tiled patios and baths, the village atmosphere and the bare sunbaked hills all around give the feel of another world lost in time.

Elegant Archena

Just 20 minutes away from here, sitting on the lush riverside in the Segura valley, are the baths at **Archena**, which knew glory in Roman times and later belonged to the Order of St John of Jerusalem. They are geared up to serious pampering – marble pavements set the tone – and are unbeatable for atmosphere and setting, but are tailored to three-week courses of treatment under medical supervision rather than a lazy morning of self-indulgence. Nonetheless the spa complex now boasts a year-round swimming pool under a glass bubble for those who want a quick dip in the waters (10am–10.30pm; entrance fee; swimming cap obligatory).

A final option is **Fortuna**, sedately functional rather than elegant, but the outside world drops away once you are immersed in the deep marble baths. The waters themselves are said to be some of the best in Europe. Treatments – everything from nasal douches, needle showers and water massages to mud baths – are so reasonably priced that you can afford to try any of them, but since the baths are open in the mornings only it's best to telephone in advance (tel: 968 685 011).

If you want to stay in the area for the afternoon, the nearby **Saladar del Ajauque** has a plethora of rare plants and a profusion of birdlife.

Right: Mula's emblem

19. ORIHUELA AND LORCA *(see map, p52–53)*

Orihuela is a 30–40 minute drive from either Murcia or Alicante. You need a full morning to see its old centre. Allow 2–3 hours to explore Lorca (an hour's drive away).

Orihuela and Lorca belong to that peculiarly Spanish breed of historic towns in which everyday life ticks over, apparently unaware, against a backdrop of stunning architecture. Buildings crumble away. Opening times are maddeningly erratic. But it is this very lack of self-consciousness, the way in which tourism plays second fiddle to local life, that gives these towns such resonance.

A Rich Heritage

The old quarter of **Orihuela** (**Oriola**) runs around the left bank of the river under the prow of the sierra. The aged buff-stone provincial shops and back-streets, the palm forest on the edge of town and the crumbling palaces and the glassy river provide the backdrop to the monumental centre.

There is the town's credentials explain its rich heritage: an independent capital in the 8th century; the launching pad for Ferdinand and Isabella's final assault on Granada in 1492; a wealthy Renaissance university and cathedral city; commercial focus of the fertile lower Segura valley. Its political power faded only in the early 19th century, when Alicante took over as regional capital and five of its monasteries were dissolved. Today, despite its fame as the birthplace of Miguel Hernández, shepherd and radical poet who died in prison after the Civil War, it remains a deeply conservative *castellano*-speaking town, looking more to the past than the future.

There is space here to describe only a few highlights. One is the **Colegio de Santo Domingo** (Tues–Fri 9.30–11am, 11.30am–1.30pm, 4–7pm, Sat–Sun 10am–2pm) on the edge of town – turn immediately right under the arched **Puerta de Crevillente** (called the angels' gate) at the end of the town's palm forest. The proportions of its cloistered patios spell out its importance first as a convent and later as a university (1610–1824). Now it is a private school run by the bishopric. You are unlikely to gain access to the church, but you can see the tiled frieze in the former refectory and the panelled and coffered

main staircase. The birthplace of Miguel Hernández is nearby in Calle Miguel Hernández (Mon–Sat 10am–2pm, 4–7pm, Sun 10am– 2pm only).

Another highlight is the shadowy **Cathedral**, an inspired small-scale patchwork of styles varying from Romanesque and Catalan Gothic to baroque. Below the vaulting, defined by spiral ribs, there is fine Renaissance ironwork, a rich 17th-century carved choir, an ornate baroque organ and, in the sacristy, Velázquez's wonderful *Temptation of Saint Thomas*. This is only the most famous among many interesting, if often unidentified, paintings in the museum (Mon–Sat 10am–1.30pm, 4–6.30pm; visits to the tower at 11am, 12.30 and 4.30pm). There are many other curiosities too, such as the 16th-century brass Virgen del Cabildo, made for versatility and economy with two detachable heads and pairs of hands to change her character. Opposite the Cathedral, right on the river itself, stands the 17th-century **Palacio Episcopal**, with its very fine cloister.

Further along the river stands the church of **Santas Justa** and **Rufina**, its gargoyled clock tower marking the southern boundary of Catalan Gothic. Beyond the Renaissance **town hall** and the **Palacio Rubalcalba**, where the tourist office and a good bar are located, is the small underground **Museo de la Muralla** presenting a stretch of the Muslim city's wall, and the **Church of Santiago** (Mon–Sat 10am–1.30pm, 4–7pm Sun 10am–1.30pm only), its carved Isabelline portal bearing the yolk and arrows of the Catholic kings. Inside, the Gothic austerity is broken by rich altarpieces by Salzillo, the Murcian sculptor whose lyrical realism has come to define Spanish baroque. More of his work can be viewed in the **Museo de Sémana Santa** in the Iglesia de la Merced, where the town's *pasos*, processional sculptures for Holy Week, are kept (Mon–Sat 10am–1pm, 5–7pm, Sun 10am–1pm only).

The best central eating place is **Los Barriles** (Calle Sal 1, tel: 966 742 365). Here there is a wonderful combination of the rice so typical of Alicante and vegetables of the Murcian *huerta*.

Faded Beauty

Like Orihuela, **Lorca** is more than the sum of its parts. The old town, running down a gentle slope, is another world, quietly faded in some parts, crumbling away or abandoned in others. It grew up as a Roman highway stop on the Vía Heraklia linking the mines of Jaen to the port of Cartagena, then became military capital of Teodomiro's independent Visigothic state and later

Left: the cathedral cloister at Orihuela
Above: detail, Iglesia de Santiago, Orihuela

the south murcia region

a strongly defended frontier city between Muslim *taifas*. Hence its oldest buildings are civic rather than religious: a Roman milestone (originally found in Plaza San Vicente), the castle keep and the Porche San Antonio, a medieval city gate.

But, as in Orihuela, the overall feel is Renaissance and baroque, the result of a building splurge after the reconquered town had been slowly repopulated by Catalans and Aragonese. Close to the central Plaza de España, you will find turrets, elaborate shields, cornices, lanterns and carved doorways decorating Italianate aristocratic houses, the granary and the town hall. **San Patricio**, the largest of the town's churches – so called because Alfonso X took the town from the Moors on St Patrick's day – looms up in lofty splendour behind its baroque façade. Its 17th-century paintings include a black Christ. Among the town's other 10 churches, **San Francisco** particularly merits a look (most are not left open during the day).

Over the past decade, the old town has undergone a major overhaul intended to inject new life into it. Houses are being restored with traditional balconies and *palominas*, or outside hanging larders. It has also become one of the main crafts centres of Spain, with an excellent **Centro Regional de Artesanía** (Mon–Fri 10am–2pm, 4–7.30pm;5.30–8pm in summer) built on Calle Lopez de Gisbert, next to the Iglesia San Mateo. Here you can examine the best selection of local crafts in the region, most notably the famed embroidered wool and silk used to dress the figures of the Semana Santa processions; these are on show all year round in two small museums – at Santo Domingo church and at Calle Nogalte 7 – run by the main brotherhoods. There is also a good range of the ceramics and pottery – clearly Muslim influenced – of the towns of the Sierra de Espuña.

Above: Lorca's castle
Left: angel statue in Lorca

Apart from this there is an interesting **archaeological museum** (Plaza de Juan Mureno s/n; Tues–Fri 11am–2pm, 5–8pm; weekends 11am–2pm; July and Aug Tues–Sun 10am–2pm). There are now plans to link all these sights to the Muslim and Christian **castle** above by a small tourist train which will start close to the river at the Convento de la Merced. For the more independently-minded, an 8-km (5-mile) walk to the river is signposted from the castle to the Cejo de los Enamorados.

20. THE SIERRAS DE ESPUÑA AND MORATALLA
(see map, p52–53)

It is 1½ hours from Alicante (45 minutes from Murcia city) to the start of the Sierra de Espuña's pine forests; another hour to the furthest point, Moratalla and its sierras.

Unlike the Andalucian sierras, the rocky massifs of Murcia have no place in travel literature or the romantic imagination. Yet the mountains, the tail end of the same chain, are quite as beautiful as anything further west, dropping from forested heights to crumpled chalky hills and villages which have kept the architectural stamp of their history as frontier towns with Muslim Granada.

This semi-circular route for a two-day foray (but allow three to four for serious walking) starts at **Alhama de Murcia**'s castle ruins and thermal baths. Just beyond, at **Totana**, where flowery glazed ceramics are made, turn off for **Aledo**, stopping off at the sanctuary of **Santa Eulalia** (always open in daylight hours). A small gem with a *mudéjar* coffered ceiling, its 17th-century frescoed cartoons tell the story of a child martyr persecuted by the Romans (outside is a bar). Aledo itself was an important frontier town belonging to the Order of Santiago from the 13th to the 15th centuries, and has tremendous views and the remains of its Muslim **fortress**.

Mountain Sanctuary

A few kilometres along the same road is the entrance to the **Reserva Nacional de Sierra de Espuña**, one of the largest nature reserves in Spain. It protects a vast area of pine forest, replanted on bare slopes in the late 19th century to stop flooding in the villages below, and flora and fauna that includes over 250 plant species, mountain cats, wild boars, native tortoises, white squirrels and rare butterflies.

The eastern exit of the park opens onto the road to **Pliego**, which runs through vineyards, almond and olive groves to meet the main road to **Mula**, a historic small town sheltering under splendidly sited castle ruins (Muslim and restored in the 16th century). It keeps a clutch of churches, traditional potters and aristocratic palaces, one of which houses the **Museo de El Cigarralejo** (Calle del Marqués 1; Tues–Sat 10.30am–2pm, Sun and holidays 10.30am–1pm), a small but stun-

Right: Hermitage, Santa Eulalia

ning museum where you can see the extraordinary finds from a nearby Iberian burial site. Here the dead were buried with their possessions and messages to the gods in large ceramic pots after cremation in a funeral pyre; these funeral trousseaux have allowed an unprecedented reconstruction of everyday Iberian life.

The road runs west from Mula to Moratalla through **Bullas** *(see page 58)*, **Cehegin** and **Caravaca de la Cruz**. A frontier town from the 11th to the 15th centuries, Caravaca is riddled with medieval mythology woven around the Knights Templar. Up in the **hermitage** built inside the **castle** you can see the church window where, it is said, angels flew in with a four-armed cross in front of the Muslim king, who promptly converted to Christianity. A bejewelled reproduction is kept in the museum (10am–1pm and 4.30–7pm;

closed Mon and Sun). The hermitage itself has a marble façade influenced by colonial or Latin baroque, a splendid quotation out of context here. In 2003 the hermitage will celebrate its first official pilgrimage year, recognised by the Papacy like that of Santiago de Compostela, to be celebrated on a seven-year cycle. Below, in the old town, wander down the pedestrianised **Calle Mayor**, take a look at the 16th-century **Iglesia de la Concepción** and, if you have time, drive out of town to see the Roman Temple and Bronze Age site at **La Encarnación**. The **Fuentes de el Marqués** is a beauty spot just outside town, with a quiet stretch of river, caves, a nature study centre and a good restaurant.

Romantic Village

Moratalla, the seat of the Order of Santiago for centuries, is something of a textbook fairy-tale village: backed by forested slopes, its streets wind up, as if around a snail's shell, to the 14th-century castle (the key, said to be the original, and torch for the dark tower, are kept at a nearby house). From here, the views over the fruit orchards and folded hills are splendid. The largely Gothic **church** is open only for morning and evening Mass.

From Moratella the road to the **Ermita Rogativa**, will take you into the highest land of the province, populated only by scattered *cortijos*, or farmhouses in the Andalucian style. Much wildlife remains and, if you take binoculars and are lucky, you may see some of the Iberian peninsula's last herds of mountain goats.

If you have a third day, you could stay overnight in Moratalla and take the road down to **Lorca**, turning off at **La Paca** to see the Argaric village at **Coy** and/or, just before you get into Lorca, to see the famous dams of **Puentes** and **Valdeinfierno**, built in the 18th century. The herby scrubland here is good walking country and from Lorca it is a quick drive back to Murcia city.

Above: mountains above Moratalla

21. CARTAGENA CITY *(see map, p52–53)*

A morning in Cartagena's museums and old town can be extended with a trip through mining country to an unspoilt beach.

Cartagena is one of the most frustrating of all historic cities. Its site, one of the safest natural harbours of the Mediterranean, speaks of its past greatness, and untold archaeological riches lie below its modern bourgeois overcoat. Yet to the casual visitor's eye the past is little in evidence, and curiously little is made of the rich cultural heritage under the surface.

Part of the answer lies in the city's extraordinary history. For an entire millennium, this was a key Mediterranean metropolis under the control of the Iberians, Phoenicians, Greeks, Carthaginians and Romans in turn. 'New Carthage is by far the most powerful of all the cities in this country,' wrote Strabo, the Roman historian, 'adorned by secure fortifications, by walls handsomely built, by harbours, by a lake and by the silver mines…'

Yet this very wealth of resources and strategic siting made the city too desirable for its own good. Stripped of its surrounding forest by the Carthaginians and Romans in order to supply fuel for the mines – Hasdrubal, Hannibal's brother extracted 300lb of silver a day – and razed to the ground in the 7th century by the Visigothic king Sisebuto, it has never found the same glory again. Many of its great buildings were used as a source of stone in later centuries and, to add insult to injury, periodic wartime battering and functional defensive rebuilding have, over the centuries, relentlessly eroded the traces of its past.

Today the city is initially unprepossessing, dominated by its naval dockyards, modern development and industry – around the corner, at Escombreras, is the largest oil refinery in Spain. But the historic core of the city and harbour area is gradually being revealed under the ramshackle streets built over it in later centuries. Even so there is much work to be done; the site of the Roman Capitol remains a grassy hillock in the centre of town (the Molinete).

Above: children playing in Cartagena

City Sights

A good place to start is the ruined **Castillo de la Concepción**, the Roman castle, above the magnificent harbour spread below. To the north lie the bullring, built over the Roman amphitheatre (currently being excavated), and the naval hospital, now a university. From the castle you can walk down into town past the ruined **Catedral Vieja**, which is thought to be one of the oldest churches in Spain and has a Roman mosaic in the crypt, and the **Roman theatre**, discovered in 1987 and now almost entirely excavated. Nearby is the **Byzantine Wall**, on show under an excellent contemporary art gallery (corner of Calle Dr Tapia and C. de la Soledad; Tues–Sat 11am–1.30pm, 5–8.30pm, Sun 11am–1.30pm). A similar basement excavation, this time of a Roman street, can be seen under Calle Duque 29 and neighbouring buildings (open during banking hours; free). Guided tours are available to all the Roman sites; enquire at the tourist office.

The **Museo Nacional de Arqueología Marítima** (Dique de Navidad; Tues–Sun 10am–3pm; closed Mon and holiday afternoons) houses finds from shipwrecked boats, and a full-scale replica of a Roman galley. The **Museo Arqueológico Municipal** (Calle Ramón y Cajal 45; Tues–Fri 10am–1pm and 4–6pm, weekends 10am–1pm), built over an important necropolis, has an excellent collection that reflects the long overlap between Iberian and Roman cultures. Smaller naval and artillery museums are pointers to the city's continuing role as a naval and military base.

Cartagena's other strong suit is some wonderful modernist architecture, paid for, as in earlier centuries, by mining wealth; much of this dates from the years 1895–97 when a new grid of streets was laid out. About half of this was destroyed in 1960s redevelopment, but some interesting stuff remains nonetheless, most of it clustered along the axis of the Calle Mayor: the **town hall**, the splendid **casino**, and the casas **Cervantes**, **Pedreno** and **Llagostera**.

The **Gran Hotel** and house at No. **27** on **Calle Jara**, the **Palacio de Aguirre** in the **Plaza de Merced**, and the **train station** are other good examples. These modernist buildings, and tombs in the splendid cemetery of **Nuestra Señora de los Remedios**, are heavy with allegory and symbolism, much of it Masonic – said to have been handed down from the mysterious Knights Templar.

The pedestrianised heart of the old town has wonderful old-fashioned shops and lots of atmospheric bars and restaurants (such as **Columbus** at Calle Mayor 18, **La Casa Tomas**, Plaza Lopez Pinto 8, or **La Tartana** *see page 76*). Afterwards, the drive eastward past the mines towards **Cabo de Palos** can be linked with a trip to the unspoilt beach at **Calblanque** *(see page 69)*.

Left: modernist architecture in Cartagena

22. CABO DE PALOS AND THE MAR MENOR
(see map, p52–53)

The road east from Cartagena travels through beautiful country to Calblanque, a natural park enclosing virgin beaches, salt lakes and rocky heights. Cabo de Palos has fish restaurants and the Marine Reserve.

The highway running east from Cartagena to the **Mar Menor** would never suggest the wild sierra and coastal landscapes lying just to the south. In the distance floats the highrise horizon of La Manga, on the sandbar built up over thousands of years to form the Mar Menor, or 'small sea'. But just a few kilometres away, the road to Portman takes you into another world.

In the empty, mournfully beautiful ochre and tawny hills that run down to the incongruously-named **Portman**, the Phoenicians, Romans and 19th-century fortune hunters drew huge wealth from silver, lead and gold mines. Today all that remains are the mining chimneys and old-fashioned machinery down by the port, called Portus Magnus by the Romans, which is now silted up by mineral residue. Dumping was halted in 1990, but a final solution has not yet been found to clean the shoreline. Nonetheless the bay, overlooked by its lighthouse, has its own rugged beauty.

Inland at **La Unión**, the small 19th-century capital of the mining country, modernist buildings include the **Antiguo Mercado Publico**, the venue for an annual flamenco festival dedicated to the songs that grew up here among the Andalucian mine workers, and the **Museo Minero** housed in the 19th-century Liceo de Obreros (or Workers' Lycée). It explains the mineralogy, history and mining processes used here for over a thousand years.

The next turning as you head east on the highway leads to **Calblanque**, a 250-km natural park that contains gloriously unspoiled sandy and rocky bays, salt-lakes packed with birdlife, rocky peaks and a few remains of the old mines. There is an information centre close to the park's entrance.

To the Cape

At weekends locals stream past here to the fish restaurants *(see page 75)* at **Cabo de Palos**, a small village with old-fashioned villas clustered around fishing boats bobbing in the port. Specialities here are *calderó*, the local fishermen's meal of rice cooked in stock followed by a plateful of fish baked in a salt crust. The high salt and iodine content of the Mar Menor's warm sheltered waters are said to give the fish its richness of flavour. Today they are as busy with watersports as fishing boats, and are protected as a Marine Reserve. With a new Nature Centre on the Paseo del Puerto organizing two guided visits a day (tel 968-145939) and underwater access, this is a divers' paradise to be enjoyed while it lasts. For those who prefer to stay above the water, there are tailor-made boat trips to the Islas Hormigas or Pedrigueras (tel 968-564532 in advance).

Right: fishing remains an important industry in the Mar Menor

Leisure Activities

SHOPPING

Spain is no longer the budget holiday destination it once was, so do not expect to find lots of dirt-cheap bargains, even if you buy locally manufactured items such as clothes, shoes and leather goods, which tend to be of very good quality.

The coast itself is not abundantly rich in local crafts, and those that do exist are now being gradually squeezed out by the advent of mass production. Nevertheless, there is an enticing array of local food and wine to be had. Inland areas, especially Murcia, have maintained their often Muslim-influenced crafts traditions, and they provide the most interesting souvenirs.

Most shops are open Mon–Fri 10am–1.30pm, 5–8pm, Sat 10am–1.30pm. Some bakeries and newsagents also open for a few hours on Sunday mornings. Department stores, hypermarkets and big supermarkets stay open during the siesta, so this is a good time to shop if you want to avoid the crowds.

Markets

All neighbourhoods in Spain have municipal food markets (*mercados*, 8.20am–1.30 or 2pm), which are often the best places to buy fresh produce. General street markets (*mercadillos*) are best for buying items such as rope-soled sandals (*alpargatas*), relatively cheap clothing, household goods such as *paella* pans, etc. Try your hand at bartering – you may be surprised by your success.

Murcia also has travelling craft markets that move from town to town on Sundays.

Alicante/Alacant

Thur, Sat, 8am–2pm. Campoamor (near Pl. de Toros). Street market ranging from fruit and vegetables to clothes.
Daily, particularly evenings. Paseo Gadia. Particularly good for jewellery, leather goods, cheap watches, etc.

Altea

Tues, 8am–1.30pm. By the port. Very tourist-orientated; cheap jeans, pearls from Mallorca, etc. A few local goods.

Calpe

Mon–Fri, 5–7.30pm. Electronic fish market. The old-fashioned 'Dutch' auction, conducted in person, has been replaced by an electronic system that utilises modern technology, such as digital screens. This market is a lot of fun because it's fast and exciting, like a stock exchange.

Dénia

Mon, 8am–2pm. By the railway station. Almonds, raisins, fig cake, etc.

Játiva/Xàtiva

Tues, Thur mornings. Pl. del Mercat. A good mixture of small country stalls, as you might expect to find in an inland, agricultural, market town.

Murcia

Daily. Pl. de las Flores. Flower market.
Dec. Christmas crafts, including wooden nativity figures (Avda Alfonso XII).

Left: produce of the plains
Right: fish is a local staple

Santa Pola
Tues–Sat, 5–6pm. At the port. Auction of fresh fish direct from the boats. Stalls outside also sell fish in small quantities.

Torrevieja
Fri. Huge street market.

Local Crafts
The following towns are known for particular local products:
Abarán: *esparto* grass mats
Agost: pottery
Alcoi: sugar-coated almonds
Crevillente: glassware, rugs and carpets, wickerwork and *esparto* grass
Dénia: raisins
Elche: shoes
Elda: shoes and lace
Gata de Gorgos: cane and basket work
Guadalest: leather goods, shawls, lace work
Ibi: toys
Jijona: *turrón*
Murcia city: carved figurines
Valencia city: fans
Villajoyosa: chocolate
Lorca hosts a fair of regional crafts in Sept.

Agost
Pottery: Museo d'Alfarería, C. Teulería 11, tel: 96 509 1199. Closed Mon. Good range, pots from Biar. At the Tibi entrance to town are **Pedro Molla** (traditional functional items) and **Emili Boix** (decorative, modern ceramics). All sell traditional white earthenware water bottles *(botijos)*.

Alicante/Alacant
Ceramics: V. Pascual, Avda. Alfonso Sabio 15, tel: 96 514 0139. Painted pottery.
Espadrilles: Alpargatería Ortega, C. General Primo de Rivera 12, tel: 96 521 4853. Sandals.
Turron: Turrones Teclo, C. Mayor 23, tel: 96 520 1115. *Turrón* and other confectionery.
Cartegena: Centro Regional de la Artesanía, Avda, Ciudad de la Union s/n, tel: 968 524 631

Elche/Elx
Shoes: Artesana del Calzado, Carr. Murcia–Alicante km 53, tel: 96 667 5441. Watch the shoes being made. Also lots of factory outlets on the N340.

Gata de Gorgos
Cane and Wickerwork: A string of shops selling furniture, baskets and mats.
Guitars: Guitarres Cashimira, C. Estación 25. Handmade items at good prices.

Jalón/Xaló
Wine: Bodega Cooperativa Virgen Pobre, Carr. Xaló–Alacalí s/n, tel: 96 648 0034. Good reds, rosés and sweet *mistela*. Mon–Fri and Sun mornings.

Jijona/Xixona
Turrón: **Museo de Turrón El Lobo**, C. Alcoi 62, tel: 96 561 0225.

Jumilla
Wine: Bodegas San Isidro, Carr. de Murcia s/n (on road to Yecla at La Alquería), tel: 968 780 700. Best known for red wines.

Lorca
Crafts: Centro Regional de Artesanía, C. Lope Gisbert s/n, tel: 968 463 912. Permanent exhibition hall and two for temporary displays as well as archives of local crafts.
Embroidery: Joaquín Castellar, C. Corredera 35. Workshop based on local tradition of lace and embroidery.
Pottery: Lario Marin, Carretera Murcia 23, tel: 968 468 183.

Murcia
Carved figurines (*belenes*):
Manuel Nicolás Almansa, C. Belenes 12, Santiago el Mayor, tel: 968 255 858
Artesanía Hnos. Griñán, Calle de la Iglesia, Puente Tocinos, tel: 968 302 211
In the 18th-century style. Two of 12 or so *belén*-makers still working in the studio.
Crafts: Centro Regional de Artesanía, C. Francisco Rabal 8, tel: 968 284 585. Fine cooperative for local crafts; workshop prices.

Villajoyosa/La Vila Joiosa
Chocolate: Chocolatería Buana, Avda. País Valencia 10, tel: 96 589 1006. Buy solid chocolate to take away, or stay for hot chocolate and *churros*. Also **Chocolatería Valor** in the same street.

Right: *arroz abanda* – the fisherman's favourite

EATING & DRINKING

Local Cuisine and Produce

The cooking of eastern Spain is the produce of the plains – oranges and lemons, almonds, orchard fruit, rice and a range of vegetables – which differentiates the local cooking from that elsewhere on the Mediterranean coast. Lighter than Catalan cuisine, it benefits from Muslim influences.

Good regional cooking is traditional, so there is no need to look for named restaurants. You just need to know what to choose in bars and cafés, markets and bakeries.

Rice is the great common denominator. *Paella*, which originated in Valencia as poor country food made with rabbit and snails, is the most famous local dish, but it is only one of the vast family of *arroces* (rices), and is often the worst choice in restaurants as it tends to be tailored to tourist expectations. Don't be put off by humbler combinations – they can be the most delicious. From the coast come *arroz abanda* and *caldero*, both made with stock from the small rock fish that fishermen could not sell in the old days; on the plains, vegetables and pork products flavour various *paella huertanos* and *arroz con costra*; in the mountains, *arroces serranos* are typically flavoured with snails, herbs from the sierras and local game such as rabbit.

Fish dishes are widely available inland, but are usually at their best in ports. Dénia's monster prawns and *arroz abanda*, Santa Pola's *gazpacho de mero*, a fish stew served on flatbread, Cabo de Palo's salt-baked fish and grey mullets' roe (*huevos de mújol* – a Mediterranean caviar) – all gain from on-the-spot freshness and local know-how. Shellfish is generally good if it's local, but falling catches have sent prices sky-high. Guardamar's *langostinos*, for example, can cost up to £50 a kilo. These days genuine *salazones* or salted fish products such as *mojama* (salted tuna), products of a tradition that goes back to Phoenician times, have also become luxuries as have the prize local hams.

Inland, especially in the sierras, traditional cooking is often more Castilian than Mediterranean. Humble dishes such as the *migas* based on breadcrumbs, *gazpachos*, shepherds' game-and-poultry stews served on top of a flat bread (which originally served as the plate) and *trigo picado*, a cracked wheat stew, are worth trying.

In the Alicante mountains, the cuisine becomes more warming: soups, stews (*ollas*) and other dishes based on dried beans, *bacalao* (salt-cod) or cured meats, cooked with saffron and the herbs of the sierras. The most famous of these are *olleta* and *giraboix*, and *pericana*, griddled salt-cod seasoned with dried peppers, garlic and olive oil.

The four main vineyard areas – Monóvar and Gorgos valley in Alicante; Jumilla, Yecla and Bullas in Murcia – are especially strong on these robust country dishes. Both Jumilla and Valencia DO (Denomination of Origin) wines are rising stars – reasonably priced red wines influenced by New World styles and organic methods.

On the fertile plains, the most varied, sensual and highly coloured cooking is that of

the Murcian *huerta*. Typical seasonings here are green garlic and *pimentón* – sweet paprika derived from local *noria* peppers. The most original dishes use the huge range of locally grown fruit and vegetables. Further north, in Alicante, *coques*, first cousins to Italian pizzas, use the same Mediterranean vegetables on crispy, thin pastry crusts. Also typical of the *huertas* are sausages made with sweet pork and poultry fattened on fruit and corn, *pasteles* (meat pies), *relleno* (rissoles), and honey from the Alicante *huerta*.

As rice is to savoury dishes, so oranges, lemons and almonds are to sweets. Oranges and lemons appear in huge mounds on roadside stalls (only buy in season), in fruit tarts and as glacé fruit; almonds are used in cakes, biscuits, puddings, liqueurs and sweets. *Turrón* nougat is wolfed down by the locals in great quantities at Christmas, and candied egg yolks *(yemas)* are also seductive.

Refreshing summer drinks and ices are another local speciality that, like many local traditions, is said to be inherited from the Muslims. When you buy an ice cream, a *granizado* (icy slush made from lemon, orange or coffee) or *horchata* (an addictive chalky, semi-frozen nut-milk made from ground *chufas*, plus sugar and water), look for a sign that declares it to be *fabricación propia* or *artesanal* (handmade). For the local wines, or *vinos de país*, which can be found in most restaurants, see the chapters with the relevant itineraries and options.

Eating Out

In general, eating out is cheap, varied and cosmopolitan near the coast. The following selection of places to eat concentrates on good local cooking.

Complaints: As is the case in many hotels, restaurants here often make a complaints book available for comments by dissatisfied customers. For example, you might order a mineral water only to find that it is not the real thing.

Opening Times: Holidays and closing times vary wildly. A lot of restaurants that are not in or near major tourist centres are closed on Sunday evenings (or even all day in city centres) and for one to two months during the summer or autumn. You should therefore phone in advance to check that your choice of eatery is open. Standard kitchen hours are 1pm–4pm and 7.30pm–midnight (occasionally until 11pm).

Most Spaniards do not eat lunch until as late as 2pm; and dinner is usually at about 10pm, but restaurants in tourist centres are accustomed to people eating earlier than this and have adjusted their times accordingly.

Payment/Tips: Prices may or may not include IVA (VAT); either way it is usual to give a 10% tip if you are happy with the meal and the service.

Restaurant Grading: Restaurants are graded in four classes (plus de luxe), but the grading often refers to the décor, the number of dishes on the menu and the price of the set tourist menu, rather than the quality of the food and service.

Snacks: If you want a light meal, many bars and *cervecerias* serve a selection of *tapas* (small dishes of tasty snacks eaten with a drink). They come in three sizes: *pinchos* (a mouthful, sometimes offered free), *tapas* (enough to fill a saucer), and *raciones* (a small plateful). Pay when you have finished (not after each item).

Vegetarians: Although Spanish restaurants do not generally cater for vegetarians, you can nearly always get a plain *tortilla* and salad, or a selection of vegetable *tapas*. Two recommendations for vegetarians are: El Girasol, Calle San José 22, Murcia, tel: 968 212 965 and L'Indret, Calle García Morato 5, Alicante, tel: 96 521 6614.

Left: a selection of *tapas*

Recommended Restaurants

Restaurant prices are graded as follows:

$ – Inexpensive
$$ – Moderate
$$$ – Expensive

Alhama de Murcia (central Murcia)
El Chaleco
Avda Bastarecte 9
Tel: 968 630 104
Great modern and traditional dishes in a sleek setting. Closed two weeks in Aug. $$

Agres (northern Alicante)
Pension Mariola
Calle San Antonio 4
Tel: 96 551 0017
Large country dining room. Local dishes. Closed 1–15 July, 1–15 Oct. MC, DC, V $–$$

Alicante/Alacant (city)
Aldebarán
Muelle del Poniente
Real Club de Regates
Tel: 965 123 430
Smart poolside eatery with local and international cuisine. MC, DC, V, AM $$

Dársena
Muelle de Levante 6
Tel: 96 520 7399 / 520 7589
Closed Sun evenings, Mon in summer. Great rice dishes and good fish. More relaxed at dinner than lunch. MC, DC,V, AM $$$

La Goleta
Explanada de España 8
Tel: 96 521 4392
Seafood and rice. MC, DC, V AM $$

Nou Manolín
C. Villegas 3
Tel: 96 520 0368
Tasty regional dishes and *tapas*. Great cellar. Good value. MC, DC, V, AM $$–$$$

Alteá (central Alicante)
Posado San Miguel
Calle Conde de Altea 24
Tel: 96 584 0143
Family restaurant on coastal road; terrace backs on to the beach. Great traditional dishes such as rice cooked over a wood fire. MC, DC, V $–$$

Bañeres
Venta El Borrego
Ctra Villena-Ontenienle km18
Tel: 96 656 7457
Traditional inn for herby mountain *gazpachos* and game stews. MC, DC, V, AM $

Benidorm
Aitona
C. Ruzafa 2
Tel: 96 586 7090
Don't be put off by the gigantic *paella* pan signboard. Locals rate this city-centre restaurant for its various local rice dishes – for example, with squid and cauliflower – and wood-grilled meats. MC, DC, V, AM $$

La Rana
Costera del Barco 6
Casa Antig (or smaller branch at La Raneta, C. Martinez Oriola 25)
Good for *tapas* that can be eaten on their own or built into a meal. Quality produce, very central. MC, DC, V, AM $–$$

El Molino
Ctra Valencia km123
Tel: 96 585 7181
Inn ambience, good food, summer terrace. Closed Mon and 1 Oct–1 Nov. MC, DC, V, AM $$–$$$

Cabo de Palos (central Murcia)
La Tana
Paseo de la Barra 33
Tel: 968 563 003
Closed Mon except in summer. Good for *caldero*, sea bass in salt. MC, DC, V, AM $$

Caravaca de la Cruz (central Murcia)
Caballos del Vino
Ctra de Murcia km63
Tel: 968 702 219
One of the Sierra de Espuña's few restaurants with lots of local dishes. Open all day. Accommodation. Closed Sat. No cards. $

eating & drinking

Cartagena
La Tartana
Puerta de Murcia 14
Tel: 968 500 011
Lunches, suppers, tapas next to the old town.
Regional, modern food. MC, DC, V $–$$

Castalla (southern Alicante)
Meson El Viscayo
Camino La Bola s/n
Tel: 96 556 0196
Specialities include mountain *gazpachos* and
home-made breads. Farmhouse ambience
MC, DC, V $

Cocentaina
(northern Alicante)
Paraje San Cristóbal
Estación del Norte
Tel: 965 650 072
Classics include *olleta*, roast lamb, *pericana*,
orange tart and home-made *aguardientes*.
Also international menu. Closed Mon, Sun
evenings in winter. MC, DC, V $$

Dénia
El Pegolí
Baret de Les Rotes
Tel: 96 578 1035
Family restaurant featuring a set menu of
giant prawns, *arroz aband*a and fresh fruit,
or fish and shellfish. If full, try El Trampoli
or Mesón Troya. MC, DC, V, AM $$$

El Algar (Murcia coast)
Los Churrasios
Avda Filipinas 13
Tel: 968 136 028
Splendid local dishes like mullet roe. $$–$$$

Elche/Elx
Restaurante Arlequin de Elche
Pl. del Congreso Encaristico 17
Tel: 965 420 160
Inn opposite cathedral. *Arroz con costra* and
other local dishes. Great value. $

Els Capellans
Porta de la Morera 14
Tel: 96 545 8040
One of three restaurants within the Hort del
Cura Hotel. Gracious, smart. Imaginative
hybrid of international and local cuisine,
such as palm-heart salad and sweet date
omelette. MC, DC, V, AM $$–$$$

Gata de Gorgos
(northern Alicante)
Corral Del Pato
Partida Trossets 31
Ctra Jalón km1
Tel: 96 575 6834
A converted farmhouse run as a family
restaurant that offers excellent local
cooking. Closed 23 Dec–end of Jan. MC,
DC, V $–$$

Jalón/Xaló (northern Alicante)
Terrases de la Torre
Ctra Gata de Gorgos-Xaló km5
Tel: 96 573 3204/575 6446
Country Alicantino food: pickles, rice
dishes, game, sausages, etc. Oct–Apr open
Fri–Sun only. Closed 1–15 July. $–$$

Játiva/Xàtiva (Valencia)
Fonda Casa Floro
Pl. del Mercat 46
Tel: 96 227 3020
Good country food, packed on market days.
Arroz al horno and *gazpachos*. Lunch is the
main meal. Closed Aug. $

Jumilla (north Murcia)
Casa Sebastián
Mercado de Abastos
Avda. de Levante 6
Tel: 968 780 194
Closed first two weeks in Aug. Breakfast
and lunch until 4.15pm. Solid provincial fare
complements cellar's 18,000 bottles. $–$$

Lorca (southwest Murcia)
Cándido
Plaza Juan Moreno
Tel: 968 466 907
Country fare. 365 days. MC, DC, V, AM $

Los Puertos de Santa Barbara
(Cartagena)
María Zapata
Carretera General s/n
Tel: 968 163 030
Great menu of lost local dishes, home-made
cheese and organic vegetables. Good wine
list. Closed Sun eves and Mon. MC, DC, V $$

Murcia (city)

Alegría de la Huerta
Plaza de San Juan 1
Tel: 968 217 481
Popular regional dishes and tapas. $–$$

El Corral de Jose Luis
Pl. Santo Domingo 14–15, Murcia
Tel: 968 214 597
Busy central restaurant with a wide range of fine local *tapas* and sit-down meals. Good value. Also try **El Churra,** Avda Maqués de los Vélez 12, tel: 283 400. MC, DC, V $$

El Rincon de Pepe
Plaza Apóstoles 34
Tel: 96 212 239
Murcian specialities. Closed Sun eves. MC, DC, V, AM $$–$$$

Raimundo González
Plaza Raimundo González 5
Tel: 968 212 377
Murcian specialities. MC, DC, V, AM $$

Pinoso (southern Alicante)

Alfonso
Pl. España 4
Tel: 96 547 7820
Country restaurant known for its *serrano*, with local white snails and roast garlic. Closed Aug. MC, DC, V, AM $–$$

Santa Pola

Batiste
Peréz Ojeda 6
Tel: 96 541 1485
Classic, classy restaurant overlooking the harbour with local seafood dishes and a good selection of meat. Closed Sun eves. $$–$$$

Meson del Puerto
Pérez Ojeda 31
Tel: 96 541 1289
Good value fish joint, with *gazpacho de mero* – fish stew served on flatbread – and *caldero*. Closed mid-Dec–mid-Jan. MC, DC, V, AM $$

Sax (central Alicante)

Meson el Almendros
Palacio de la Fuerte
Tel: 96 547 5032
Good charcoal-grilled fish, lamb and other

local dishes. Handy for the Madrid–Alicante motorway. Closed two weeks in Aug and Sun eves. MC, DC, V, AM $–$$

Tàrberna (northern Alicante)

Casa Pinet
Plaza Mayor
Tel: 96 588 4229
Country cooking in lighthearted political atmosphere. Excellent *olla*. $

Torrevieja (southern Alicante)

Las Canàs
San Policarpo 13
Tel: 96 571 5248
Popular for fish, seafood and rice. Good value. Open 365 days. MC, DC, V, AM $–$$$

Miramar
Po Vista Alegre s/n
Tel: 965 571 3415
Classic waterfront eatery with seafood, fish baked in salt and rice. Closed Nov and Tues Oct–Mar. MC, DC, V, AM $$–$$$

Vall D'Ebo (northern Alicante)

Bar Piscina
Polideportivo Vall D'Ebo
Tel: 96 557 1475
Great home cooking, both local and Frencht. Lunch served all year round; dinner mid-June–mid-Sept or to order during the winter. Closed Thurs. No cards $–$$

Villajoyosa/La Vila Joiosa

El Pachel
Partida de la Ermita 28
Tel: 96 589 0003
Fresh seafood and fish dishes – alternatively try the inexpensive restaurants down by the fishing quarter. MC, DC, V $–$$$

Right: lunch with a view

NIGHTLIFE

When night falls, the Costa Blanca and Costa Cálida have something on offer for everyone, and there is enough entertainment to keep you going all night – if that is what you are after. In July and August, most Spaniards desert the inland towns and go on their holidays. As a result, many of the coastal resorts are somewhat lifeless out of season. In summer, the night train that runs from Alicante to the resorts, goes all the way to Dénia.

Discos, Pubs and Bars

Discos and Spanish-style pubs get going around midnight, and some stay open until breakfast time, so make sure you have a good siesta. Dress is usually casual, but you might well be sent home to change into something more formal if you turn up in shorts.

Pubs, which are nothing like English pubs and would be better described as young people's bars with music, don't have entrance fees, and during the week you probably won't have to pay to get into discos either (especially if you're female). However, at weekends there may be an entrance fee. Drinks in both discos and pubs are pricey, but spirit measures are very large.

Bars are open from breakfast time until the early hours of the morning. It is usually cheaper to sit at the bar than at a table.

Alicante, Benidorm, Torrevieja, Lo Pagán and Murcia are the busiest nightspots.

Alicante/Alacant

During the summer, the action is in **San Juan** as well as Alicante itself. Wander along the seafront market (6pm–2am) and enjoy the cafés. **Penelope** and **Filly** are the two main discotheques. Other pubs offer pop music, videos, swimming pools, game machines and pool tables. **Night Fever** is the most popular disco with the under-25s. The municipal Plataforma Cultural is an open-air stage for live music that is open throughout the summer.

For a summer night's entertainment with a more native flavour, start with a drink on the **Explanada**, and then go to Alicante's old town near the cathedral. This is where the bars are concentrated. **La Missión**, **Hanoi** and **Nazca** have rooftop terraces. You can listen to good jazz music in stylish **Desafinado** (just off the Rambla) or admire the imaginative décor in **El Forat**. Across the Rambla, **Calle San Fernando** has a host of young people's clubs. **Doña Pepa**, by the town hall, is a classic dance hall for the older generation. Other alternatives include the Nochas del Castillo (dinner and live show) at weekends in July and August, the slick bars such as **Di Roma** and the modern complexes at either end of the harbour, and **Varadoro de Villamartin**, a techno disco just outside Alicante.

Benidorm

In summer, every night is party night; in the winter, Benidorm really comes alive only at weekends. The old pedestrian quarter is

Above: the party goes on throughout the night

the scene of many bars and cafés. **Eros** (Calle de la Santa Faz) is a small, supposedly gay bar that is actually patronised by a mixed clientele. The main central disco is **Black Sunset** (Calle Esperanto s/n). For pubs and discos with a difference, head just out of town to the N332. You cannot fail to miss **Ku** (open summer only), a 'spaceship' equipped with bars, disco, helicopter and swimming pool. Avoid **Penelope** – the biggest disco in town – and **KM**, unless you enjoy 'Miss Topless' and 'Miss *Camiseta Mojada*' (wet T-shirt) competitions and other entertainment designed to appeal to the package tourist. Back in town, **Conuco** (Avda Europa) offers salsa dancing – with classes too – and there is also square and sequence dancing, tangos and *copla* in many hotels.

A little further towards Valencia, a discreet signpost announces **L'Anouer** (open all year), a small, up-market bar with roguish churchy-baroque décor. There is a romantic garden in which candles illuminate secluded tables and pious statues.

Lo Pagan

The summer resorts here have become a new nightlife centre: **Sal Gorda**, in Santiago de la Ribera, is a good café at which to start the night. The clubs – **El Barracón**, **Apalache** and **Pasaje** – are located in the street behind the church and are open midnight–5am while Sirocco in Lo Pagan has good live music on Thurs and Fri. The main discotheque area – **Penelope** and others – is on the road to San Pedro del Pinatar.

Murcia city

In the university area, **El Ahorcado Feliz** and **La Puerta Falsa** (for live music) are good bars; the Teatro Roma is surrounded by bars catering to an older crowd; **Misa D6** is a classic club-disco opening at 6am (Ctra Sta Catalina s/n).

Torrevieja

In the summer, open air cafés and ice cream parlours fill the streets around the port; later the bars and clubs open. Various pavement artists, a funfair and a market (summer, 7pm–1am) add colourful characters. Classic bars, apart from the Casino in the port, are the **Casablanca** and **María Sarmiento**. In winter, Torrevieja is busy only at weekends.

Other places

On the coast, **Altea's** old quarter (behind the beach) is full of bars and restaurants. **La Plaza**, next to the church, has live music on Thurs. **Birimbao** and **El Passat-xe** are other popular bars. In both **Calpe** and **Dénia**, the action takes place along the beach – winter weekends and summer only. The busiest area in **Cartagena** is the **Cuesta de la Baronesa** (near the cathedral), where there are many pubs and cafés; other areas include the **Calle Cuatro Santos** and **Calle Bodegones**. In **Santa Pola**, the bars in the town centre (near the port) cater mainly for the younger generation. Among the good discos are **Camelot**, **El Cano** and **Bolero**.

Elche's entertainment is situated in the heart of the town, whereas **Orihuela's** is practically non-existent. Alcoi is generally pretty dead in July and Aug, but the **Santa Rosa** district and also the area around the **Pl. España** perk up a bit in autumn.

Shows

For glorious tackiness, you can't beat the expensive extravaganza at the mock castle, **Castillo Fortaleza de Alfaz**, tel: 966 865 592, 7kms (4 miles) from Benidorm just off the N332 to Altea. A mediocre medieval banquet features jousting and duelling. The chamber of horrors leads up to a futuristic disco with its multiple video screens and lasers. **Benidorm Palace**, tel: 965 851 660, on the eastern outskirts of town, is reminiscent of a tacky show hall. Catering with a vengeance for the international crowd, it offers 'Spanish style' cabaret and the occasional one-off concert (Julio Iglesias started his career at the Benidorm Palace).

Casinos

You won't de admitted without showing your passport (minimum age 18). Dress is casually smart. The casinos are used to informal tourists and do not have a strict dress code. **Benidorm**: **Casino Mediterraneo** (tel: 965 890 700), 5kms (3 miles) from Benidorm on the N332 towards Villajoyosa, open all year 8pm–4am; entrance fee; drinks at pub prices. Games featured include blackjack,

chemin de fer and roulette. Cash dispenser in the foyer for credit cards and Eurocheques. 300 ptas entrance fee.

Murcia: There is a luxury casino in Calle Apóstoles 34.

The Gay Scene

The main centre is **Benidorm**, which has everything from exclusive hotels such as **Villa de los Sueños** (tel: 96 586 88 24), through a string of restaurants, saunas and bars for a mainly gay clientèle, although heteros might enjoy the relaxed atmosphere. Restaurants include **Hierbas** and **Secret Garden**; a bar tour could include **People, Mercury, Orpheo's** and **The Look**. A good starting point in Alicante is **Canibal Shop**, Colón 16, a book, clothes and perfume shop; **La Mission** is a good restaurant and bars include **Missing** and **La Cúpula Azul**. Venues in Murcia include the **Piscis** bar and **Metropol** club. Venues can be contacted through the No Te Prives association, tel: 968-295484. In **La Manga, Papagays** (Ctro Comercial Las Dunas) is the main gay bar.

For Culture Vultures

Theatre and concerts: There are three theatres in **Alcoi**, two of which also show films. All are in or near the **Pl. de España. Elche** and **Murcia** each have one theatre, of which the more important and lively is the **Teatro Romea** in Murcia. Murcia also has good concerts year round in the Auditorio (Avda

1ro Mayo). Many towns have a **Casa de Cultura**, where concerts and other cultural events takes place. The local savings banks also have auditoriums that host a variety of events, often free.

Most musical performances are grouped in seasons or festivals; the most important of these are the **International Music, Dance and Theatre Festival** (July–Sept), the **International Jazz Festival** in Murcia (the week after Easter), **La Mar de Musicas** open-air world music festival in Cartagena (July), and **Festival Nacional de Cante de las Minas** (Aug) in La Unión, Spain's most prestigious annual flamenco cycle.

Zambra, a *tablao* in Campello, hosts good year-round **flamenco** shows (weekends only in winter, tel: 965 632 310).

Cinemas

There are cinemas in the large towns, as well as summer open-air and drive-in cinemas in the coastal resorts. The **Astoria**, in the *barrio* **Sant Cruz** in **Alicante**, occasionally shows English-language films in the original print. Many cinemas offer cheap tickets on a particular night of the week.

Bullfighting

Spaniards discuss endlessly whether this is a sport, a stylised art form or a barbarian form of torture. You will have to decide whether the sight of a bull being gradually weakened for the kill is for you.

The standard of bullfighting in the region is generally high, especially in **Alicante** (the best time is at the end of June) and **Ondara** *(see page 23)*. There are other bullrings in **Benidorm, Cartagena, Murcia** (best in the first week of Sept) and **Torrevieja**, as well as occasionally installed temporary rings in other tourist centres which feature displays by junior *toreros*.

Ticket prices vary considerably between and within each bullring, depending on the quality of the *toreros* and on where you sit. It is worth paying the extra to sit in the shade during the summer and also to hire a cushion, because the spectacle lasts about 2½ hours or more. Be warned that an agency will charge up to 20 percent more than the standard price, and a hotel will charge up to 40 percent more.

Above: the Costa Blanca is the place for some Mediterranean passion
Right: for aquatic thrills and spills, take your pick from one of five coastal water parks

SPORTS & ACTIVITIES

For Children and the Young at Heart

There are five **water parks** along the coast (at Benidorm, Torrevieja, Santa Pola, Rojales and La Marina), where you can spend a day sliding and splashing about. Take sensible precautions against accidents – fatalities have been known to happen at water parks.

Local **boat rides** go from Jávea (Jun–Sept), Calpe (around the Peñon d'Ifach, summer only), Benidorm (to the island, all year) and most of the Mar Menor resorts (to the islands in the centre, summer only). Sailing boats can be chartered for a privately tailored expedition. If you want to take a more detailed look at the local marine life without getting wet, hop aboard one of Benidorm's **glass-bottomed boats** *(see also ferries, page 92)*.

Boats tour the **Río Safari Elche** (tel: 965 638 288) outside Santa Pola. There are two local **safari parks**: **Vergel** (tel: 965 750 285) near Pego, and **Aitana** (tel: 965 529 273) at Penáguila, 35km (22 miles) inland from Benidorm, which is the biggest wildlife park in Europe. You can also see animals at **Fort West**, a Wild West theme park near Campello, and at **La Nucia**'s small cowboy town and zoo. Benidorm's **Mundomar Marine and Exotic Animal Park** (daily 9am–6pm) features what it claims is Europe's biggest dolphinarium. The dolphins perform morning and afternoon. For **balloon rides** from Elche, tel: 96 663 7401.

For children's fairgrounds, **Festilandia** in Benidorm and **Festival Park** in Calpe are good, but are rarely open in winter. Kids will like Guadalest's museums of miniatures, **Mundo de Max** and **1,001 Curiosities**.

Go-karting is available at many places along the coast. For fun on smaller wheels, go **roller-skating** (rinks at Xàbia, Calpe, Benidorm and Alicante).

If weather conditions force you indoors, try Alicante's **Museo de Belenes** (Museum of Nativity Scenes; Calle San Agustín 3; Tues–Sat noon–2pm, 4.30–7.30 or 8pm in summer; small admission fee) or Ibi's impressive toy museum (Tues–Sat 10am–1pm, 4–7pm, Sun 10am–2pm).

Watersports and Fishing

The warm calm Mediterranean is a paradise for watersports enthusiasts. The Mar Menor, immediately south of the Costa Blanca, is particularly noteworthy. If you don't have your own equipment, hire it on the beach or from a nautical club.

Windsurfers and small **sailing** dinghies may be hired on many beaches, but La Manga is best for the serious windsurfer or sailor. Calpe is the only place for **parasailing**. If the wind drops, hire a **speedboat** at Benidorm or **jet skis** at Dénia or Xàbia (Jávea) and let an engine do the work.

Water-skiing, available at many resorts, is an expensive sport to try. Check beforehand the length of the run, the permitted number of falls, and possible discounts for multiple runs. A cheaper alternative is **cable skiing** off the Playa de Levante in Benidorm.

You could also move under your own steam in a **pedal boat**, or try canoeing inland at Beniarrés dam.

The Amadorio dam (near Villajoyosa) and Guadalest dam are good places for freshwater **fishing**. You will need to obtain a licence from the appropriate government department, the *Consellería d'Agricultura i Pesca*, C. Professor Manel Sala 2, Alicante (tel: 96 593 4000). Ask for details in a tourist information office or fishing-tackle shop.

Local fish include *barbel* (carp), bass and rainbow trout.

Under the Water

Snorkelling and **sub-aqua** are excellent in certain areas that have protected the submarine flora and fauna that thrives on the sea grass *(Posidonia oceanica)* that grows in patches on the sea floor. Popular haunts include the Playa de Barraca (southeast of Xàbia), the Peñón de Ifach (Calpe), Playa de Torres (just east of Villajoyosa), Cabo de las Huertas (San Juan), the Cabo de Palos (La Manga) the islands of Benidorm and Hormigas – both now registered as marine reserves – and Tabarca, which still has the odd turtle swimming offshore.

For **sub-aqua**, a diving centre can usually provide a diving permit (also available from the *Consellería d'Agricultura* as above), equipment, a boat, tuition and tips about the local area. Alicante has more than 30 diving schools and the Mar Menor 12. For contacts ring the Federación de Actividades Subacuaticos, tel: 968 215 141, or try www.acuc.es/valencia.htm

Snorkellers who swim away from the shore must tow a marker buoy, for safety reasons. Watch out for sea urchins, wear flippers or plastic shoes when snorkelling or swimming near cliffs and rocks, and be careful where you put you hands.

If your accommodation does not have a swimming pool, inland towns such as Elche and Murcia have a public outdoor pool, and most large towns have an indoor one.

On Land

There are **caves** at Benidoleig (Ondara), Canalobre (Buslot) and Vall d'Ebo. Experienced riders can go **horse riding** in the mountains. Novices may have to make do with lessons in the paddock. For details of all these, ask in tourist offices.

Cycling is now popular: tourist information offices can supply information on hiring bikes and routes graded by difficulty.

Golf courses are open to visitors on payment of green fees and most clubs hire out equipment. The new 18-hole course at Playa San Juan, Alicante was designed by Severiano Ballesteros; there are another 18 courses in the province. El Club de la Manga is the most famous Murcian course. For all golf details, tel: 965 846 213 or 284 832.

Hotels with **tennis** courts often let non-residents play for a fee. At Villajoyosa, Eurotennis (tel: 96 589 1250) is a three-star hotel/apartment complex specialising in tennis holidays. Many towns have tennis clubs open to non-members.

Walking, Climbing and Nature Reserves

Various mountain ranges, nature reserves and sierras offer **walking and mountaineering** to heights of 1,500m (4,875ft). Major areas include the Sierra de España to the south, and the sierras within the triangle formed by Alcoi, Dénia and Benidorm.

Calpe has the 333-metre (1,000-ft) Peñón de Ifach. A system of numbered Pequeños Recorridos (PRs), none of which are longer than 50 km (31 miles), are well signposted throughout the Alicante countryside. They range from walks through the Sierra Helada above Benidorm to coastal rambles from Santa Pola. For further information, tel: 902 100910.

The **Walkers' Train** (Trenet Senderista, tel: 96 526 2731) offers guided walks along the Dénia to Alicante route on Wed and weekends. Other interesting areas to explore are the Barrancos del Infierno and Mascarat, the Sierras d'Aitana, and de Mariola in the northern hill ranges, the Guardamar Dunes and small Murcian sierras (Yecla, Jumilla, de la Muela and Villafuerte) further south. The Cueva del Puero (tel: 968 745 162) has 11km (6½ miles) of tunnels, galleries and caves.

Left: the region attracts growing numbers of walkers

BEACHES

This is a brief, selective guide to help choose a beach *(playa* or *platja)*, either for a quick visit in combination with one of the itineraries or for a long, lazy day's sunbathing and swimming. It includes Costa Cálida and Costa Blanca beaches.

The Costa Blanca falls into two halves: the northern bays and coves from Dénia to Alicante (divided by rocky headlands and backed by mountains), and the flat shoreline stretching south from Alicante to the regional border with Murcia and the Mar Menor.

There are some unspoilt beaches in the north: the rocky inlets of **Les Rotes** south of Dénia; the **Mar Azul** opposite **Portitxol**, the **Playa de Granadellas** and **Cala de los Tiestos** on the Cabo de la Nao; the coves north of Calpe, such as **Fustera** and **Pinets**, pebbly **L'Albir**, north of Benidorm, **Cala Tío Ximo** (Benidorm), and the bays south of Villajoyosa, such as **Cala del Xarco**. Many can be reached by rail as well as by road.

In Alicante, **Postiguet**, the city-centre beach, has a more local feel than **San Juan** or **La Albufereta**; the badly signposted **Cabo de la Huerta** has defied development and is good for snorkelling off the rocks.

South of Alicante, beaches are emptier and the development less continuous, but the high-rise resorts and villa estates stand out more brutally against the flat landscape. **Los Arenales**, within close range of Elche, has ugly apartment blocks, but a good stretch of gently sloping sand for children. **Tabarca**, Santa Pola's island, is inundated in summer because of the breeziness of its small beach, but its coves have some of the most interesting sub-marine life of the whole coast.

Of the other beaches between here and the Mar Menor, **La Marina**, backed by pine forest, is good for shade, and **El Carabassí** just north of Santa Pola is protected from development. **Dehesa de Campoamor** (a 20-minute drive from Orihuela) has kept some unspoilt coves below rocky cliffs.

San Pedro del Pinatar, the first main Murcian resort, marks a shift to the warm, calm shallows, greyish sand and largely Spanish family tourism of the inland Mar Menor resorts. They are quietest between Los Alcázares and Los Nietos, where you can look over to the long sandy spit of **La Manga**, which is filled by traffic in summer. **Las Matas Gordas** is a narrow spit where the Mar Menor almost meets the Mediterranean. The finest beaches are around the corner. Known collectively as **Calblanque**, they have glassy-clear water, skin-diving and a rare wide horizon of undeveloped coast protected as *parque natural*.

South of Cartagena, **Calnegre** and **Cabo Cope**, which have been protected from development since 1994, are wild stretches of coast with small coves. **Bolnuevo** and **Azohía** are friendlier sandy beaches.

Nude Sunbathing

Women's topless sunbathing on the main beaches of the Costa Blanca and Costa Calida, is normal, and unlikely to offend locals. Nude sunbathing is permitted on: **Ambolo**

(Cabo de la Nao), **Los Judíos** (Cabo de Huertas), **El Saladar** (south of Alicante city), **El Carabassí** (Elche district), **Los Tósales San Juan** (Guardamar), **Calblanque** (Murcia), and **La Marina** in **Portús** (just south of Cartagena).

Blue Flags

Costa Blanca and Costa Calida beaches have a good record – 44 have been awarded EU 'Blue Flag' standards for cleanliness, safety and amenities – more than any other coast. Busy beaches have lifeguards, Red Cross posts and sometimes rescue boats. A green flag means the water is safe, a yellow flag means swimmers should be careful and a red flag means sea conditions are dangerous.

Above: the Playa del Postiguet, Alicante's city-centre beach, has a local feel

CALENDAR OF FIESTAS

Fiestas (*festas* in *Valenciano*) fuse historic traditions with regional customs. There are now so many fiestas, both small and large, that it is impossible to list them all. This brief calendar has a bias towards traditional popular culture and fiestas that are hospitable to outsiders. The dates of many move with the religious calendar. Get details from tourist offices or town halls.

5–6 January

Los Reyes Magos: Epiphany eve sees parades in towns all over Spain celebrate the arrival of the Three Kings. In Aledo and Cañada (near Villena), there are *autos*, or religious plays, on 6 Jan.

17–19 January

San Antón: Typical rural festivities – the blessing of animals, horse-and-cart parades.

Mid-February–Lent

Carnaval: The Iberian carnival, originally a pre-Lent feast, has returned in a wild, secular way in the past 20 years, with costumes – a lot of them transsexual – dancing through the night, big street parades and lots of drink.

Holy Week

Semana Santa: The processions all over Spain between Palm Sunday and Good Friday have interesting fervent rituals. Those in the Murcia region are known for their processional images and baroque pageantry.

Particularly noteworthy (with days of the major processions indicated where relevant) are: Callosa de Segura (Wed and passion play on Good Friday); Cartagena (Wed, Fri, Sun); Crevillente; Elche (Palm Sunday procession in the town where all the Easter palms come from); Jumilla (Tues, Sun); Lorca (procession famed for the rivalry of the two brotherhoods, Azul and Blanco, on Good Friday); Mula and Moratalla (with *tamborada* drumming Wed, Thurs, Fri); Murcia city (Los Coloraos, Wed; Silencio, Thurs; Los Salzillos, Fri); Orihuela.

April

Fiestas de Perimavera (Spring festivals in Murcia city and the surrounding villages). A cross between a huge horticultural show and a folklore festival, with the most traditional elements being the *Bando de la Huerta* – dancing, singing and satirical flower-laden floats – and the *Entierro de la Sardina* (literally 'Burial of the Sardine'), marking the end of Lent.

Pentecost Sunday

Festa del Xop (Planes): This is the oldest fiesta of Alicante province which, it is traditionally believed, guarantees fertility; a poplar tree is uprooted and planted in the main plaza and then scaled by the village's bachelors.

Above: effigies are burnt on St John's Night during Hogueras de San Juan in Alicante city

April–September

Moros y Cristianos (Alcoi, April 22–24; Caravaca, early May; Jijona, late Aug; Lorca, Sept; Orihuela, late July; Villajoyosa, end of July; Villena, early Sept): Centuries-old and typically Alicantino, these fiestas commemorate the Christian reconquest with parades of elaborately costumed Muslims and Christians and a mock battle – leading to a Christian victory of course. Lots of bangs, gunpowder and fireworks along the way. Alcoi's fiestas, on St George's Day, are the best known for their sumptuous costumes and atmosphere. At Caravaca de la Cruz, the *Caballos de Vino* is a horse race based on the famous occasion that the Knights Templar broke the Muslim siege to fetch drinking water.

May or June

Corpus Christi: Religious processions.

Late June

Hogueras de San Juan (Alicante city): The most famous and popular of the city's fiestas, with effigies burnt on St John's Night after a week of all-night street parties and live music. The fiesta dates from the 1920s, but the tradition of fire festivals on summer solstice is pre-Christian. Midnight fireworks over the bay follow the *Nit del Foc*. Smaller *Hogueras* take place around the same time in Jávea, Dénia, Benidorm, Calpe and Pego.

Mid-July

Fiesta del Carmen (Tarbarca, San Pedro del Pinatar and other Mar Menor villages, Villajoyosa): The main fiesta of Spanish fishing ports. Images of the *Virgen del Carmen*, the fishermen's saint, are carried round the harbour and/or taken out to sea to bless the decked-out fleet.

Santísima Sangre (Dénia): These fiestas include a battle of flowers and the *bous en la mar*, in which bulls are released on the quayside – either they or their human persecutors fall into the sea.

Mid-August

Fiestas de la Vendimia (Jumilla): a week-long fiesta celebrating the grape harvest. The town fountain runs with wine.

September

Fiestas de Cartagineses y Romanos (Cartagena): similar to the *Moros y Cristianos* but this fiesta celebrates the expulsion of the Romans from the city.

ARTS & CULTURAL FESTIVALS

Mid-August

Certamen Internacional de Habaneras y Polifonía (Torrevieja): The rhythmic choral *habaneras* were brought to Spain by 19th-century sailors and exporters from Cuba. A week-long programme. For tickets tel: 96 571 2570.

Late August

Festival Nacional del Cante de las Minas (La Unión): Founded as recently as 1960, this festival preserves flamenco mining songs, which were introduced to the region by immigrant Andalucian mine workers. Held every year in the wonderful modernist market building, this festival is now ranked along with the most important flamenco events in Spain. Tickets are available from tourist offices.

Early September

Festival de Folklore del Mediterráneo (Murcia): This festival highlights a different country each year, but there are always participating groups from all over the world.

Right: re-living the Reconquest

Practical Information

GETTING THERE

By Air

Both British Airways and Iberia operate scheduled flights to the Costa Blanca. If you can be flexible about your departure date and time, you should be able to pick up a cheaper charter deal to Alicante; as a general rule, the longer you wait to buy your ticket, the cheaper it will be. A number of companies such as Easyjet and Spainair operate cut price flights.

The area has three airports: El Altet (tel: 96 691 9000), 10km (6 miles) to the southwest of Alicante; Manises (tel: 96 370 9500), 15km (9 miles) west of Valencia; and San Javier (tel: 968 172 000), on the coast 40km (25 miles) to the southeast of Murcia.

Transport to and from Airports

Some international car-hire firms have branches at the airports where you can collect or hire a car.

A taxi ride from **El Altet airport** to the centre of Alicante takes 15 minutes. Buses run to and from town every 20 minutes between 7am and 9.20pm; the journey time is roughly 40 minutes. There is a bus between the airport and Elche every two hours.

A bus runs between Valencia bus station and **Manises airport** at hourly intervals between about 6am and 9pm; allow 45 minutes for the trip.

From **San Javier airport**, you will need to get a taxi to San Javier town, then a bus to Murcia. The bus leaves once every two hours and the journey takes one hour.

By Boat

There are two direct car ferry routes from Britain to Spain. Brittany Ferries sails from Plymouth to Santander (tel: 0990 360 360) and P&O European ferries from Portsmouth to Bilbao (tel: 0990 980 555). Both crossings take over 24 hours. Rough seas can cause cancellations in autumn and winter.

By Car

To drive from Britain to southeastern Spain will take at least two or three days or 30 hours minimum if you drive non-stop, even if you travel on the expensive French motorways. If you're driving from Santander to Alicante, you should allow 10–15 hours for the journey.

Your car must be equipped with a wing mirror on each side, headlamp deflectors, two warning triangles and a set of spare light bulbs. For peace of mind, consider taking out continental cover with a reputable breakdown service such as RACE (tel: 96 522 9349 and 968 230 266)

You will need a 'green card' (international insurance certificate), your registration document and a Spanish bail bond. This document will prevent the Spanish police from locking you up if you injure somebody in an accident. It is advisable to carry an International Driving Permit or a Spanish translation of your driving licence; some kind of licence must be carried at *all* times.

By Coach

Coach travel to the Costa Blanca is relatively cheap, but the journey – from London

via the Channel ports and France, then down the Spanish coast past Valencia and on to Alicante and Murcia – takes an arduous 1½ days, so be warned and take a good book.

By Train

Tickets for journeys between Britain and Spain can be obtained from any leading travel agents or from Rail Europe (tel: 0990

Left: Alicante port
Above: ceramic street sign in Xàbia

January and February are the best months to see and smell the pink-and-white almond blossom. During the spring months lemon and orange blossoms, and many other Mediterranean plants are in flower. If you are a birdwatcher, go in winter to see the spectacle of migrating flamingos at the saltpans and lakes along the coast south of Alicante.

Entry Requirements

British and other EU nationals, as well as nationals from the US, Australia and New Zealand need only a valid passport to enter Spain for a period of up to three months. Visitors from other countries should check with their nearest Spanish embassy.

What to Wear

Spanish people tend to dress with a casual elegance, but it is perfectly acceptable to wear scruffy or beach clothes in tourist areas. For the sake of decorum, you should be well covered when visiting churches, monasteries, etc. Nor is it a good idea to explore inland areas in skimpy beach wear, as this may shock older people.

848 848). Thomas Cook publishes a comprehensive European timetable, which is available from its branch offices.

Electricity

Plugs have two round pins. Voltage is 220 AC. A converter and/or an adaptor plug may be useful if you want to take electrical appliances with you.

TRAVEL ESSENTIALS

When to Go

The Costa Blanca, protected by mountain ranges, enjoys a mild Mediterranean climate with year-round sunshine, low rainfall and moderately high humidity. July and August are uncomfortably hot, with temperatures reaching 35°C (95°F) on a regular basis. The coolest months of the year are January and February, when temperatures range from a low 7°C (44°F) to a pleasant 17°C (63°F). These also tend to be the wettest months of the year, along with March and April.

Thick, heavy clothes are unnecessary, even in winter. In summer, light clothes made from natural fibres are preferable, and sunglasses are essential if you are doing a lot of driving.

During the summer months many banks, department stores, high-class hotels, restaurants and public transport vehicles are air-conditioned. In winter some hotels and restaurants, particularly in the higher, cooler regions, are centrally heated.

The sea temperature is ideal for bathing from April to early November, although braver swimmers can be spotted taking a dip in winter.

Time

Spain is one hour ahead of Greenwich Mean Time (GMT) in the winter, and two hours ahead in the summer. In January, the sun rises at about 8.15am and sets at about 6pm; the corresponding times in June are 5.45am and 8.15pm, although the light lingers for another two hours.

GETTING ACQUAINTED

Crowds

July and August are the peak months for tourists, both Spanish and foreign. This is a good time if you like lively coastal resorts. However, if you are looking for a peaceful holiday and want to avoid inflated prices and traffic jams, especially at the beginning and end of August and for the holiday week-

Above: freshly baked in Benissa

end (14–15 August), you are advised to stay away from the coast during this period.

Fiestas

At all times of year you are sure to find a fiesta or an arts festival somewhere *(see Calendar of Fiestas)*. If you value your sleep, make your base outside the town and travel in for the festivities (but remember that roads in the centre are often closed to non-residents). Sightseeing can be frustrating at fiesta time: it is hard to make your way around, and shops and museums may be closed.

Please note, too, that fiesta and festival tickets are usually available only direct from *ayuntamientos*.

Language

English is spoken by many people, as you would expect in a major tourist area. However, you will probably find a phrase book useful, and it is worth learning at least a few basic expressions before you go. A small effort on your part will help you to make friends with local people.

Attitudes to Tourists

British tourists do not have a very good reputation on the Costa Blanca as a result of the behaviour of *los hooligans*. However, the Spanish emphasise that the offenders are not only British, and locals often tend to be surprisingly friendly.

Attitudes to Children

The Spanish dote on children, and they are sure to be given a warm welcome wherever they go; hotels are very understanding about their needs and will do their best to provide meals to suit.

You are unlikely to find a babysitter except by means of an informal personal arrangement, but it is part of the Spanish way of life for children to accompany adults to cafés, restaurants and fiestas, even very late at night.

Religion

Roman Catholicism is dominant throughout Spain, but only Anglican and Evangelical churches have Christian services in English (see local English-language press for

details). There is a scattering of Jehovah's Witness churches throughout the area, as well as a synagogue in Benidorm and Buddhist temple in Benimantell.

Visiting churches can be tricky because, unless they are major landmarks, they are generally open only at the times of Mass, i.e. early morning and early evening, and all Sunday morning. At other times, or for smaller churches, you usually need to ask for the priest *(cura)*, who may be available to give you the key and/or show you around. Monasteries and convents are open all day; ring the doorbell to be admitted.

Sex

There is a large divide in Spanish attitudes to sex: part of the population has become liberal since Franco's death, as a cursory glance at Spanish TV will confirm, while others remain dogmatically conservative. Legally, the minimum age for sex, both heterosexual and homosexual, between two consenting people is 15. All contraceptives are available at chemists, and condoms can be bought at supermarkets.

Harassment

Some women experience unwanted attention from local men. Historically, the Spanish have perceived foreign women as more likely than Spanish ones to be available for sex. On the whole, it is quite safe to travel alone, but if you are on the nervous side you may want to consider taking a personal alarm with you.

MONEY MATTERS

Although the Euro was declared Spain's official currency in January 1999, all monetary transactions will be carried out in pesetas until 2002. Coins are produced in 1, 5 (a *duro*), 10, 25, 50, 100, 200 and 500 pesetas (ptas). Notes are available in 1,000, 2,000, 5,000 and 10,000 ptas.

Getting Cash

You can bring up to 1 million pesetas into Spain; you will need your passport to get hold of any more. Exchange rates are generally similar for cash as for travellers'

Natural History

Since the 1970s, the areas of Spanish coast and countryside protected or marked out for the value of their landscape and wildlife have increased enormously, highlighting their often overlooked importance and value. There are various categories: *parque natural* and *parque natural terrestre-marítimo* (the latter covering both sea and shore), which are the most stringently protected; *paraje natural*, an interesting landscape; *reserva de caza* and *reserva integral*, protecting the wildlife. These are marked on maps, although sometimes not very accurately, since certain proposals for protection haven't come to fruition due to opposition from local landowners and/or industry, and others are too new for the maps.

Along the coast itself, some capes and offshore islands have kept a remarkable submarine life, which flourishes on the sea grass (*Posidonia oceanica*). It used to cover the entire continental platform, but is now only left in patches. For this reason Tabarca, where it is still possible to see turtles, is a marine reserve with controlled public access. Other areas that stand out are the Islote de Benidorm and the Islas Hormigas (both recently registered as marine reserves), the Cabo de la Nao, and Calblanque, protected as an *espacio natural*. There is a project pending to make the entire Mar Menor a

reserve, but it remains to be seen whether this will become a reality.

The best known *parques naturales* within the Costa Blanca region are the pine forests of the Sierra de Espuña (the second largest *parque* in Spain) and the wetlands of the Albufera. But there are others within Alicante province: the Peñón d'Ifach, with interesting plant life, Pico del Montgó to the south of Dénia and Carrascal de Font Roja, which is an important last outpost of mixed Mediterranean woodland with *carrascas* (kermes oaks). As well as the Sierra de Espuña, Murcia region has La Valle, an area of sierras to the south of Murcia city.

The string of salt lakes down the coast were upgraded from *parajes naturales* to *parques naturales* in 1994 and are host to much interesting bird life: flamingoes, grebes, numerous species of wading birds including avocets, black-winged stilts and other migratory species – particularly numerous during the spring and autumn migrations. The Lagunas de la Mata and Torrevieja, and the Laguna de El Hondo have been intelligently transformed in recent years into ecological activity and education centres, and 250 recorded species have been observed at the Salinas de Santa Pola.

Besides this, there are areas of great beauty and interest with no special protection: the Barrancos del Infierno and Mascarat, the Sierras d'Aitana and de Mariola in the northern hill ranges and valleys, the Guardamar Dunes and small Murcian sierras (for example Yecla, Jumilla, de la Muela and Villafuerte) further south. As elsewhere in Spain, the rural areas are rich in birdlife – with colourful bee-eaters, rollers and hoopoes, larger birds such as storks and herons, and raptors including various species of buzzards, eagles and, in the mountains, Egyptian and Black vultures.

Last but not least, there are the exotic *palmerales,* or palm forests, thought to have been planted by the Phoenicians, among which Elche's municipal park and privately owned Hort del Cura are outstanding. Now that these palm trees have little commercial value other than for gardeners, there are worries that the forests, too, are a threatened and slowly disappearing part of the landscape.

Left: barn owls are one of several species of owl found in the region

cheques, and banks usually give you the best deal. A good exchange rate often means heavy commission, so shop around. If you change large sums of money at one time, you'll probably save on commission, but you'll have more to lose if you're mugged; and of course you'll have more to change back at the end of your stay.

Travellers' cheques are the safest way to bring your money, as they can be replaced if lost. They cannot, however, be used to pay for goods directly. Remember to make a note of the serial numbers and to keep this separate from the cheques.

Having money sent to Spain from abroad is complicated, expensive and time-consuming, and should be done in emergencies only. Contact your bank for further details.

Credit Cards

Many hotels, up-market restaurants and all department stores take credit cards, Visa and MasterCard being the most-widely accepted. Most credit cards can be used to obtain cash. You can withdraw money over the counter during banking hours; if you know your Personal Identification Numbers (PIN), you will have access to cash from numerous 24-hour dispensers, usually with a modest handling fee charged by your bank. If you use a credit card the exchange rate will be the one that is current when your cash advance is processed. Numbers for lost or stolen credit cards are as follows: Visa 900 974445, MasterCard 900 971235, Amex 915 720000..

GETTING AROUND

By Car

Remember to drive on the right and overtake on the left. This may sound elementary, but it is easy to forget on empty country roads.

Seat belts are compulsory. Speed limits are 60kph (38mph) in built-up areas, 100kph (62mph) on major roads, and 120kph (75mph) on motorways. Speeding fines are high and are payable on the spot. Children under 13 must sit in the back seat. Spanish law states that you must carry a spare set of headlamp bulbs and a warning triangle.

In large town or city centres, on-street parking spaces are hard to find, although expensive multi-storey car parks generally have room. Anarchic and double parking are national pastimes in Spain, but don't be fooled into thinking that the police never give parking tickets or tow cars away.

Petrol grades are super (97 octane), normal (92 octane), unleaded (95 octane) and diesel. Unleaded petrol is available everywhere.

There are two kinds of motorway in Spain: *autopista* (which you must pay a toll to use) and *autovía* (which is free). An expensive toll is levied on the coastal motorway north of Alicante (about 800ptas Alicante to Dénia, for example); there is no charge south of Alicante and on the N330 past Elda and Villena. The motorways are a good investment in summer and during the rest of the year in rush hours. These are generally linked to exoduses from towns at weekends and holidays, and influxes to town for highjinks at night and the return to work at the end of the weekends. The siesta period (approximately 3–5pm) is a good time to travel. Local roads to beaches are often congested on public holidays and Sundays in summer. New motorways from Valencia to Murcia and on to Albacete are due for completion in 2002.

An unnerving minority of Spanish drivers are impatient or love to take risks. Beware of those who ignore red traffic lights, pedestrian crossings, etc. In case of an accident, there are SOS points every 5km (3 miles) on major roads; the police emergency phone number is 091. Make sure you obtain full details from any other driver involved. Any injury, however slight, has to be reported to the police, and the injured person must be taken to hospital.

Hiring a Car

A British travel agent should be able to arrange car hire for you, but small local companies are generally cheaper than big international ones. If you're under 23 and/or you have less than two years' driving experience, you'll probably find it difficult to rent a car.

You will need your passport and an International Driving Permit (your British licence will probably be accepted). All firms charge a set fee per day, plus IVA (tax) and insurance. Some firms charge extra for mileage. A hefty deposit is usually required unless you pay by credit card.

Hiring a Moped or Bicycle

Bicycles and mopeds for hire are easy to find in coastal resorts, and relatively cheap. To hire a moped, you must be aged 16 or over and have your passport and driving licence. Spanish moped riders rarely wear helmets, but they are compulsory and should be worn for safety reasons. Mopeds use *mezcla* (mixed) petrol.

By Taxi

Taxis are good for getting around towns and are generally cheaper than in Britain. An available taxi displays either a green light or a sign saying *libre*. The meter should be running. Surcharges are added to the basic fare at night (11pm to 6am), at weekends and on public holidays, for trips outside the city and to the airport, and for luggage. Tipping (5–10 percent of the fare) is expected.

By Coach

There is no single national coach line; ask at tourist offices where you need to go for your destination. Local coach services can only be booked and paid for in Spain, and seat reservations should be made in advance. Coach stations are laid out according to the company, not the route. Alicante station, tel: 96 592 9802, Murcia station, tel: 968 292 211.

By Train

Tickets can be bought at train stations, RENFE (the Spanish railway network) travel offices or any authorised travel agency at any time between 60 days and five minutes

before departure. There are different types of train, varying in price and speed from the fast *talgo* down to the slow *exprés*.

Discount fares are available on offpeak days *(días azules)*. On production of suitable identification, senior citizens, families with children and young people under 26 can also obtain discounts off the normal price. You can buy a tourist pass valid for unlimited travel within Spain for periods of 8, 15 or 22 days. A rail guide including fares (issued monthly) can be obtained at any Spanish railway station. The relevant RENFE routes within this area are Cartagena–Alicante–Valencia, Alicante–Madrid, and Cartagena–Murcia–Albacete–Madrid. The fast Euromed service to Valencia from Alicante takes 1½ hours; Alicante to Madrid takes 3–4 hours. A high-speed line from Madrid to Valencia is due to open in 2002. For further information and reservations, tel: 902 24 02 02. Alicante, tel: 965 920 202, Murcia, tel: 968 252 572.

The FGV narrow-gauge railway *(see page 27)*, leaves Alicante from the station next to Postignet beach every hour. All trains travel as far as Benidorm, and about half complete the two-hour journey to Dénia.

In summer months, the train also runs a night service, the Trensnochador, serving the resorts and returning from Dénia in the early hours of the morning. The Lemon Express uses the same line, and runs from Benidorm to Gata and back on Saturday mornings. Reservations can be made at Benidorm station, tel: 96 585 1895. Walkers' trains run at weekends *(see pages 27 and 82)*.

By Sea

You can find out about or book the follow-

ing ferry services through any local travel agency.

Hydrofoil to Ibiza: Flebasa, tel: 902 160 180, runs daily hydrofoil services from Dénia to Ibiza, taking about three hours.

Ferries to the Balearics: Trasmediterranea, tel: 902 454 645, has regular sailings from the port of Valencia to Mallorca, Menorca and Ibiza.

Ferry to Tabarca: The shortest journey is via Santa Pola (25 minutes); this route and the one from Alicante are both operated by Kontiki, tel: 96 521 6396, running from April to November. The longest route, between Torrevieja and Tabarca, takes one and half hours and runs daily June to September. For tickets and further information, tel: 96 670 2122.

HOURS AND HOLIDAYS

Business Hours

Shops are generally open from 9am–1pm and 4–8pm Mon–Sat; in resort towns many stay open on Sundays.

Post offices are open from 9am–2pm Monday–Friday, and from 9am–1pm on Saturday.

Banks operate Mon–Fri from 8.30am or 9am to 2 pm; some branches stay open on Saturday, but close an hour earlier. They are closed on Sunday and all official holidays. Outside banking hours, you may be able to change money at a hotel, station, airport or department store.

Public Holidays

The following dates are public holidays in both Alicante province and Murcia region: 1 and 6 January, 19 March, Easter Thursday, Good Friday, 1 May, 15 August, 12 October, 1 November, 6, 8 and 25 December; 9 June is also a public holiday in Murcia; 19 March and 9 October in Alicante. Local holidays are in late April (Murcia spring festivals) June (San Juan), on the Monday of Easter week and on Thursday after Easter (Santa Faz).

If you are planning to travel to the Costa Blanca over the Christmas or Easter periods, do not worry about finding everything shut down for weeks – this is not the case.

WHERE TO STAY

Hotels

Hotels are graded from one to five stars, *hostales* from one to three and *pensiones* from one to two. The appropriate category is displayed on a blue plaque at the entrance. If you are looking for atmosphere, you can't beat the state-run chain of *paradores*. These luxury hotels are often in renovated convents or castles or, like the one in Xàbia (Jávea), modern buildings in privileged settings. At the other end of the market there are increasing numbers of bed and breakfasts and country houses to rent *(casas rurales)* appearing away from the coast.

All hotels are required to display prices (including service and tax) at the reception desk and in every bedroom, and to have a complaints book *(Hoja Oficial de Reclamaciones)* for customers' use. Any complaint must be sent to the relevant authorities within 48 hours, so a request to use the book will probably solve any argument.

Hotels will usually do your laundry if requested. You'll be lucky to find a self-service launderette outside coastal resorts.

The following list is a personal selection of hotels that have character, are in pleasant locations and are a little different from the run-of-the-mill establishments. They are all popular so its best to book ahead. The hotels have been rated as follows (prices given are for accommodation only, in a double room with bathroom, during the high season):

$ = under 5,000 pesetas
$$ = 5,000–10,000 pesetas
$$$ = over 10,000 pesetas

In Towns

Alicante/Alacant

Mediterranean Plaza (four stars)
Pl. del Ayuntamiento 6
Tel: 965 210 188
Sleek 50-room hotel in the old town with gym and sauna, close to the beach. $$$.

Pension Les Monges Palace (two stars)
C. Monjas 2–10
Tel: 965 215 046
Modernism and Mediterranean styles meet in this great pension in the old town; garage, computer lines and TV, but no restaurant. $–$$.

Left: Alicante station

Altea
Hostal Fornet (no stars)
C. Beniardá 1
Tel: 96 584 3005
Some rooms have a terrace and sea views.
Garage for extra 500ptas. $$.

Cartagena
Los Habaneros (two stars)
San Diego 60
Tel: 968 505 250
Friendly 1950s hotel, very well positioned
for exploring the old town and harbour. $$.

La Manga del Mar Menor
Príncipe Felipe
Los Belones
Tel: 968 331 234
Part of the luxurious complex La Manga
Club, built in the style of a Spanish village.
Facilities include golf courses, swimming
pools, tennis courts and a health centre.$$$

Dénia
Las Rotas (two stars)
Partida Las Rotas 71
Tel: 96 578 0323
By the sea just outside Dénia. Tennis court,
and restaurant leading out to pool (Apr–Oct).
Parking. $$–$$$

Elche/Elx
Hotel Huerto del Cura (four stars)
Porta de la Morera 14
Tel: 96 545 8040
Modern *parador* in the palm forest, includ-
ing individual chalets in an attractive garden.
Swimming pool and tennis court. Covered
parking. $$$

Lorca
Hostal del Carmen (one star)
C. Rincón de los Valientes 3
Tel: 968 466 459
Among the very few places to stay. Small,
clean *pensión* in the centre of town. Good lo-
cal cooking; on-street parking. $$. No cards

Murcia
Hotel Arco de San Juan (four stars)
Pl. de Ceballos 10
Tel: 968 210 455
Built on the site of an 18th-century palace
and retaining the original façade. Unusual
décor and many works of art; parking. $$$.

Torrevieja
Hotel Madrid
C. Villa Madrid 15
Tel: 96 571 1350
Usefully down-to-earth hotel close to mo-
torway (Crevillente turnoff) and salt lagoons.
$$.

Xàbia/Jávea
Parador de Turismo de Jávea (four stars)
Avda Mediterranea 7
Tel: 96 579 0200
Uninspiring architecture, but privileged po-
sition on the seafront. Swimming pool and
garden; garage. $$$.

Off the Beaten Track

Agres
Pensión Mariola (no stars)
C. San Antonio 4, on road into village
Tel: 96 551 0017
Plain rooms, comfortable lounge and rustic
dining room; parking. $.

Alfafara
Casa Rural El Pinet
Masía El Pinet s/n
Sierra Mariola
Tel: 96 552 9039
Founding member of rural tourism scheme;
the 18th-century farmhouse has double and
triple rooms, swimming pool, and a six-
person flat. $$.

Left: bougainvillaea adorns a typical
village street

Balneario de Archena
Hotel Termas (four stars)
Carr. Balneario s/n
Tel: 968 670 100
Access via stairs and tunnels to baths and fountains below. Very elegant. Covered parking. $$–$$$.

Bullas
Hospedería Molino de Abajo
Ctra de Totana s/n
La Vila Joiosa
Tel: 968 431 383
Idyllic and very comfortable converted watermill with horse-riding, river swimming and an excellent restaurant. $$.

Caravaca de la Cruz
Hostal-Restaurante Caballos del Vino
(one star *pension*)
Carr. Murcia km63
Tel: 968 702 219
On main road into Caravaca from Cehegin. Serves excellent food around the clock. Parking. $. No cards

Confrides
El Pirineo (no stars)
C. San Antonio 52
Tel: 96 588 5858
Good base for exploring Costa Blanca; inland but within easy reach of the coast. Homely family-run hotel, local cooking; parking. $–$$.

Moratalla
Hostal Levante (one star)
Carr. del Canal 21
Tel: 968 730 454
Outside the village centre. Family-run bar-restaurant with rooms upstairs. Parking. $.

Tabarca
Casa Gobernador (2 stars)
Tel: 965 114 260
Wonderful hotel on an island, inside a historic building, with local cooking. $$.

Renting a Villa

Self-catering accommodation is not usually rented for less than a week at a time, and usually in calendar monthly or fortnightly blocks. Characterful local houses can be

> ### No number
> The presence of s/n in a Spanish address denotes *sin número*, which translates as "without number"; such unhelpfully un-numbered buildings are normally large – hospitals, schools and large hotels.

tracked down by travelling around yourself, or phoning the regional rural tourism schemes: tel: 968 706 600 for Murcia, and 96 552 9039 for Alicante.

Camping and Caravanning
Most campsites are concentrated along the coast, and only the official sites are legal. They are classified according to prices and amenities: luxury, then first to third class. Most sites have running water and electricity. Prices, which at the more luxurious sites are similar to those of a cheap hotel, must be displayed at each entrance.

At many sites it is possible to camp all year round, although outside the peak summer months there may be fewer amenities and the site may have a slightly depressing out-of-season feel.

The following is a small selection of well-run sites open throughout the year.

Benidorm: Caravanning-Camping Villasol (first class), Camino Viejo de Valencia s/n, tel: 96 585 0422. The most central and most luxurious. Indoor and outdoor swimming pools.

Elche/Elx: Camping El Palmeral, C. Curtidores s/n, tel: 968 542 2766. In the middle of the palm forest. Swimming pool.

Moratalla: La Puerta (second class), tel: 968 730 008. Beautifully situated model campsite in forest in river valley with waterfall. Swimming pool, tennis court, barbecues, spring water. Nearby Bullas also has a good site. Also houses to rent.

HEALTH & EMERGENCIES

If you are not used to strong sun you should take precautions. In summer, sightseeing is best restricted to the early morning or late afternoon, when the heat is more bearable than it is in the middle of the day. The Spanish don't have a midday siesta for nothing!

Eating and Drinking

Not all tap water on the Costa Blanca is drinkable, and none of it has a particularly pleasant taste. Bottled mineral water, sparkling *(con gas)* or still *(sin gas)*, is readily available in shops and restaurants. Excessive amounts of alcohol or cold drinks during hot weather are a common cause of 'Spanish tummy'. Fruit and vegetables should always be washed carefully. If you are caught short, don't hesitate to use the toilets in a bar or petrol station; this is common practice because there aren't many public toilets elsewhere.

Chemists

A green or red cross sign identifies a chemist *(farmacia)*. They are generally open from 9.30am–2pm and from 4pm–8pm on weekdays, and for the morning hours only on Saturday. Outside these times, a list of on-duty chemists providing an emergency service can be found on the door of each pharmacy.

Spanish pharmacists are highly trained paramedics, and can deal with many minor ailments. You can freely buy some medicines, including certain antibiotics, that in Britain are available only on prescription.

You can get a large discount on the cost of medicines if you have a Spanish doctor's prescription; you may find it difficult to use a foreign prescription in Spain but you may buy the product at full-price.

National Health Services

If you are an EU resident and have an E111 form (obtainable from the Dept. of Social Security) you are eligible for free treatment from the Spanish national health service. For extra protection, take out medical insurance as well. Vaccinations are not needed for visitors from Britain.

If your case is urgent, ask a chemist or your hotel for directions to a public hospital *(residencia* or *hospital)*; take the original and a photocopy of your E111 form if you have one; if not, take your passport along instead.

Facilities for the Disabled

Although awareness of the needs of disabled people is increasing, facilities, such as lifts and adapted toilets are still few in number.

Crime & Emergencies

Take elementary precautions to avoid being the victim of crime. In coastal resorts and big towns, beware of pickpockets, con artists and bag snatchers. Don't sit in your car with your bag or purse on your lap; it may be snatched by thieves on a motorbike. Don't leave valuables in your car and watch your

A Note on Language

Since 1982 Alicante province has been bilingual along with the rest of the autonomous region of Valencia. *Valenciano* – now on an equal legal footing with *castellano* (or Spanish) after years of suppression under Franco – is a written and spoken language closely related to Catalan. *Valenciano* has its own literature and is now the language of local government, as well as regional television and radio. Murcia uses only *castellano*, though sometimes with the dying local dialect of *panocho*.

On an everyday spoken basis, however, the reality is more complex than this. The northern third of Alicante province remains solidly *valenciano* speaking and another wedge in the south – around Elche and the Segura valley – is rapidly becoming so now

that young people are learning *valenciano* at school. However, *castellano* continues to dominate in Alicante city, the Vinalopo valley, Orihuela and other border areas with Murcia and, of course, in many of the coastal resorts. Road and street signs, maps, local newspapers and other printed information reflect this regional shading and are not yet consistently bilingual.

As a result, *Insight Pocket Guide: Costa Blanca* is not entirely consistent either. City and town listings give both *castellano* and *valenciano* placenames where they differ (for example, Elche and Elx) and names of museums and restaurants are given as they were found. In general references within the text, both are used as appropriate to the context, although *castellano* tends to occur more frequently than *valenciano*.

possessions carefully if you are on the beach.

If anything is stolen, go to the local police station; the police are unlikely to try to find your belongings, but you will need to fill in a form for insurance purposes.

While wandering around old quarters, you may be approached by drug dealers. Drug dealing and trafficking are illegal in Spain.

Useful numbers: police line to report minor crimes, tel: 902 102 112; fire brigade 085; local police 092; national police 091; guardia civil 062; **British Consulate** in Alicante, tel: 96 521 6190); **British Consulate** in Benidorm 965 850 123; **US Embassy** in Madrid, tel: 91 587 2200.

COMMUNICATIONS & MEDIA

Post

Stamps can be purchased at tobacconists *(estancos)* as well as at post offices. Airmail to Britain takes two to ten days to arrive – less if you pay an extra charge to send it *urgente*, and you put it in a red postbox (standard letters go in yellow ones).

Telephone and Fax

Public phone boxes have instructions for use in English. There are also large telephone offices where calls are paid for after they have been made; you can make a reverse-charge call *(cobro revertido)* from these offices or from a call box. Many bars, hotels, restaurants and petrol stations have coin-operated phones. For Spanish directory enquiries dial 1003; for international enquiries dial 1025. If you wish to bring your mobile phone, contact your network for details – arrangements and costs vary widely. It may be cheaper for you to rent a mobile in Spain.

To call other countries first dial the international access code 07, then the relevant country code. If you are using a US credit phone card, dial the company's access number below, then 01, and then the country code. Sprint tel: 900 99 0013; AT&T tel: 900 99 0011; Worldphone tel: 900 99 0014. The international code for Spain is 34; the area code for Alicante and Valencia provinces is 96 and for Murcia province 968. You need to use this area code at all times even if you are phoning within a province or indeed within a small town.

You are likely to be able to fax from a printer, copy shop or stationer *(papelería)*.

Newspapers

National newspapers you might find interesting include *El País* (centre-left), *Diario 16* and *ABC* (centre-right) and *El Mundo* (unclear). The *Costa Blanca News* and the *Entertainer* are published in English and are targeted primarily at expatriate residents, as is the glossy magazine *Lookout*. They are available mostly in coastal resorts, where the international press can also be bought a day after publication.

Events Listings

These can be found in all of the publications mentioned above. Town halls and tourist offices often publicise events, and www.lanetro.com is a listings website.

English-Language Books

Don't expect to find anything other than popular fiction paperbacks on sale. Most large bookshops sell at least some English-language books: the best in Alicante is Ochenta Mundos (Marqués de Molins 65, tel: 965 200 439). There are English-language bookshops dotted along the coast, at Alfaz del Pi, Benidorm, Calpe, Dénia, Xàbia (Jávea)

and Torrevieja, where international newspapers are also available.

TV and Radio

There are two national public television channels in Spanish (Castilian): TVE1 and TVE2. There are also two private channels (Antenna 3 and Tele 5), and the subscrip-

Above: directions to the post office

tion-only Canal +. International satellite channels, including many English-language ones, are widely available in hotels and bars. The Alicante area also receives the regional television channel Canal 9, in Valencian, and TVE3, in Catalan. Murcia receives Canal Sur from Andalucia.

The BBC World Service can be picked up on a short-wave radio. Frequencies for this area are 15.070MHz/19.19m and 12.095MHz/24.80m.

Some local radio stations have a small part of their output in English: you can check the local English-language press for details.

USEFUL ADDRESSES

Tourist Information Offices

Opening hours vary, and fluctuate considerably. Most offices are open for approximately four hours in the morning and another three hours in the late afternoon. Many are open on Saturday morning. During the summer months some are open longer, and large towns often set up temporary summer offices in addition to the all-year-round ones. However, most are closed on Sunday throughout the year. Even if you are somewhere which doesn't have a tourist office, the town hall may be able to help.

General tourist information numbers are Alicante, tel: 902 100 910 and Murcia tel: 902 101 070. Websites are www.costablanca.org and www.murcia-turismo.com.

Alicante/Alacant: Explanada de España 2, on the seafront, tel: 96 520 0000; Pl. de Ayuntamiento, town hall, tel: 96 514 9251; C. Portugal 17, by the coach station, tel: 96 592 9802; Alicante Airport, tel: 96 691 9367.
Altea: C. St Pierre 9, tel: 96 584 4114.
Benidorm: Avda. Martínez Alejos 16, in the old town near the town hall, tel: 96 585 3224.
Calpe/Calp: Avda. Ejércitos Españoles 66, between the seafront and the old town, tel: 96 583 1250.
Caravaca de la Cruz: C. de las Monjas 17, tel: 968 702 424.
Cartagena: Pza Bastarreche s/n, tel: 96 850 6483.
Dénia: Plaza Oculista Buigues 9, tel: 96 642 2367.

Elche/Elx: Paseo de la Estacíon s/n, located in the municipal park, tel: 96 545 2747.
Gandía: C. Marques de Campo s/n, in front of train station, tel: 96 284 2407.
La Manga: km0, Los Amoladeras, tel: 968 146 136.
Lorca: Palacio Guerara C. Lopez Gisbert s/n, tel: 968 466 157.
Los Alcázares: Avda de la Libertad 50, in the town hall, tel: 968 171 361.
Mula: Convento San Francisco, C. Doña Eelvira, tel: 968 661 501.
Murcia: C. San Cristóbal 6, tel: 968 366 100, 366 130.
Orihuela/Oriola: C. Francisco Díez 25, near the town hall, tel: 96 530 2747.
Santa Pola: Pl. de la Diputacíon 6, tel: 96 699 2276.
Torrevieja: Plaza Ruíz Capdepont s/n, tel: 96 571 5936.
Xàbia/Jávea: Pl. del Almirante Bastarreche 24, by the port, tel: 96 579 0736.
Xàtiva/Játiva: C. Noguera 10, near the Cathedral, tel: 96 227 3346.

In England: 22–23 Manchester Square, London W1M 5AP, tel: 020 7486 8077 (9.15am–4.15pm Monday–Friday) or 0900 166 9920 (24-hour brochure request line). You can also visit the tourist office's informative website (www.tourspain.es)

FURTHER READING

There are very few other guide books or travel accounts that deal with this region in isolation. For more information, try the **Instituto Cervantes** website (www.fourlanguages.org).

Alicante y Murcia. Geoplaneta, 1999 (aerial photographs of the entire coastline).
Brenan, Gerald. *The Face of Spain*. Penguin, 1988 (first published in 1950).
Hooper, John. *The Spaniards*. Penguin, 1987.
Hooper, John. *The New Spaniards*. Penguin, 1994.
Macaulay, Rose. *The Fabled Shore*. Oxford University Press, 1986.
Pritchett, V S. *The Spanish Temper*. Hogarth, 1984.
Walker, T. *In Spain*. Corgi, 1989.

Right: fiesta flags provide decoration and shade

INSIGHT
Pocket Guides

Insight Pocket Guides pioneered a new
approach to guidebooks, introducing the
concept of the authors as "local hosts" who
would provide readers with personal
recommendations, just as they would give
honest advice to a friend who came to stay.
They also included a full-size pull-out map.
Now, to cope with the needs of the 21st
century, new editions in this growing series
are being given a new look to make them
more practical to use, and restaurant and
hotel listings have been greatly expanded.

☀ INSIGHT GUIDES

*The world's largest collection of
visual travel guides*

*Now in
association
with*

ACKNOWLEDGEMENTS

Photography	**Robert Mort** *and*
22B, 32, 38B, 82	**J.D. Dallet**
6B, 6T, 7B, 12, 29, 21, 28, 35, 50, 55,	
62, 63, 64B, 70, 85, 90	**Nick Inman**
54	**James Davis Travel Photography**
10	**Instituto Geografico Nacional**
13	**Oronoz**
7T, 16, 25, 26B, 26T, 30, 34, 36B, 36T,	
41T, 57, 61, 75, 81, 83, 87, 92	**Prisma**
14	**Jan Read**
5	**Mark Read / APA**
1, 2–3, 41B	**Robert Harding Picture Library**
86	**Topham Picturepoint**
94	**Trip / E & J Bradbury**
Front cover	**Trip / M. Feeney**
Back cover, 11	**José Martin**

Cartography	**Maria Donnelly**

The author would like to thank Alicia Gómez and Vicente Martin for their invaluable help with the updating of this book

© APA Publications GmbH & Co. Verlag KG Singapore Branch, Singapore

INDEX

index

Cova del Rull 28
Coy 66
Culebrón 45

Dehesa de Campoamor 51
Dénia 12, 22, 26–7
  shopping 71
disabled, facilities for 96

Eating out 74–7
Elche (Elx) 40, 42–3
  Alcázar see Palacio de Altamira
  eating out 76
Elda castle 49
El Spagnaletto see Ribera, José
environment and ecology 16, 50
Ermita Rogativa 66

Festivals and events 84–5, 89
  flamenco festival (La Unión) 69
  Misterio de Elche mystery play (Elche) 42
  Moors and Christians fiesta (Alcoi) 25
  Nit del Foc fiesta (Alicante) 36
Font Roja 24
Fonts de Algar 23, 29
food and drink 73–4
  nougat 38–9
  wine 15, 44–5, 57–8, 73
Fortuna 61
Fuensanta 61
further reading 98

Gallinera Valley see Vall de Gallinera
Gandía 31
Gata de Gorgos' 23, 72, 76
getting around 91, 92–3
getting there 87–8
Gorgos Valley 23
Guadalest 29–30
Guadalest Valley 29–30
Guardamar de Segura 51

Hannibal 35
health and emergencies 95–7
Hernández, Miguel 62
Hondón 45

Jacarilla 60

Javalí Nuevo 60
Jijona (Xixona) 38–9, 72
Jumilla 57–8
  eating out 76

La Mola Castle 48–9
language 89, 96
La Paca 66
La Romana 45
La Unión 69
Llíber 23
Lorca 12, 15, 63–5, 66
  eating out 76
  shopping 72
Lorcha 28

Mañar 45
Mar Menor 69
Molina de Segura 60
money matters 89, 91
Monóvar 40, 44–5
Moratalla 66
Mula 65–6
Murcia city 12, 15, 55–7, 60
  bishop's palace 55
  Casa de Andrés Almansa 56
  Casino 56
  Cathedral 55, 60
  cathedral museum 55
  eating out 76
  Iglesia de Merced 56
  Iglesia de San Juan de Dios 55
  mill museum 60
  Museo de la Ciudad 55
  Museo Ramón Gaya 57
  Museo Salzillo 56
  nightlife 79
  Plaza Cardinal Belluga 55
  Plaza de Camachos 55
  Puente Viejo 55, 60
  San Miguel church 56
  San Nicolás church 56
  San Pedro church 56
  Santa Ana church 56
  Santa Catalina church 56
  Santa Clara church 56
  shopping 71, 72
Muro de Alcoy 28
Muro del Comtat 28